27 Kisses

A unique story of four homeless families, refugees from the former Jugoslavia, who escaped to England on the last day before John Major locked the doors. Rozelle Raynes and her husband Dick, with their deep and long-standing love of Croatia and its inhabitants, made a home for the four mothers and their ten children, and took them under their wings.

This highly descriptive and moving account – tragic, heartrending but frequently amusing – in which each person is so clearly and warmly portrayed, tells how the families adapted to English life, and became integrated in a small rural community with the help of some of their neighbours and such larger-than-life characters as "Big John".

When two of the families returned to their own country, the story moves to the twilight existence they were forced to lead in war-ravaged Croatia.

27 KISSES
(The last Coach from Croatia)

Rozelle Raynes

Thomas Lyster

British Library Cataloguing in Publication Data
A catalogue record for this book is available from the British Library

ISBN 1-871482-14-3

Publisher's Note
The opinions and comments in this book are the personal ones of the author.

The front cover, maps, pen and ink drawings (apart from Ivana's drawing on p. 128) and most photographs are by the author.
The photographs on the back cover, and those on pages 5, 6, 7, 75, 118, 132, 143, 161, 184 and 185 were taken by friends of the Croatians.
Separate acknowledgement is given to Press photographs

Published by Thomas Lyster Ltd
Old Boundary Way, Ormskirk, Lancashire

Typesetting by Waring Collins Partnership
Ormskirk, Lancashire

Printed in England by Redwood Books, Trowbridge, Wiltshire

Contents

TO DICK

and our big Croatian family

Anica, Janja, Katica and Marica
and their children
Antonija, Marjan and Josip,
Dragana and Dragan,
Natali and Ivan,
Marijana, Ivana and Damir.

PART 1
ENGLAND

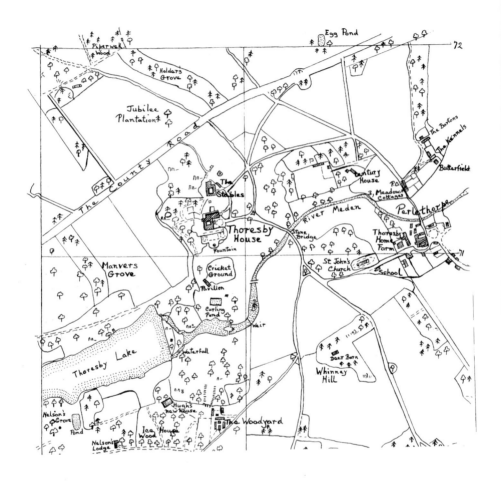

Sketch map of Thoresby Park and environs in Sherwood Forest, Nottinghamshire

Chapter 1 - A Taste of Šljivovic

"*Živeli!*" said Katica, her blue eyes gleaming with emotion behind her large plastic spectacles. She raised a glass of *šljivovic* to her lips and swallowed it in one gulp.

Živeli! (Live Long!)" we all exclaimed, savouring the fiery liquid with timid Anglo-Saxon lips. A moment of silence descended on the crowded room as the Angel of Peace moved briefly through our midst.

It was a cold November's night in 1992, and Katica was one of the fourteen refugees – four mothers and ten children – who had just arrived from Croatia to share our lives in a remote village in Nottinghamshire. Her frail old mother back at home in Krajina had pressed the bottle of home-made *šljivovic* (plum brandy) on her as a parting gift.

"Keep it till you reach some place that you can call your home," her mother had instructed her; "then share it with your hosts in the new country."

Well, there we all stood in the lamplight surrounding Katica: the coach-drivers, interpreters and helpers who had brought the women and children to England against all the odds – they were the last group of refugees to land in Dover before John Major introduced the visa to put a clamp on any further homeless people from the former Jugoslavia coming to England. Then there were Malcolm and Cynthia Wonnacott, who had worked harder than any of us to transform that 11-roomed flat into a place that you could proudly call a home. There were the four mothers – Anica, Janja, Katica and Marica – very pale and exhausted after their traumatic departure from Croatia and non-stop journey across Europe; and their ten children – eyes round as tennis-balls, drinking in their new surroundings like migrant birds just flown in from some distant land. And finally, Dick and I, who had struggled ceaselessly for the past three months towards that special moment. At last, we could offer a new home to some refugees from our much-loved Jugoslavia, the country where we had received such heart-warming friendship and generosity in bygone years.

*   *   *   *   *   *

The seed was first sown some twenty-six years ago in a village called Brusje on Hvar Island in Jugoslavia. It was early in March with the sky grey and threatening, and the mountains covered with flowering rosemary, heather and broom.

"Is there a café in the village?" I asked an old woman who was gathering firewood, as I was tired and thirsty after our long climb up from Hvar Town.

"No, there is not," she replied gruffly, peering at us with cautious black eyes. "Follow me!"

She led us to a grey stone house with green shutters and a tiled roof, and bellowed "Matice!" as we approached the door.

A young woman with chestnut-brown hair and a broad smiling face ushered us into a spotless white-washed kitchen. "Be seated," she said, "and I will make you some coffee."

Dick had brought with him his latest toy, a Polaroid camera; and it proved to be a small miracle in Brusje. The kitchen rapidly filled with grandfathers and grandmothers, uncles and aunts, the village school-master and a steadily increasing throng of close friends and neighbours. And, quite suddenly, into their midst strode Jakov, a huge bear of a man with a mattock slung over one shoulder and a black beret planted four-square on his head,

"What is the cause of all this commotion in my kitchen?" he demanded in a thunderous voice. His eyes rested without pleasure on his womenfolk, then swivelled to Dick who appeared to be at the centre of the disturbance.

"*Dobar dan!*" my husband ventured, holding out his right hand to Jakov who pulverized it in a grip of iron.

Luka, the youngest child, ran forward, holding up his photograph for his father to see. Silence fell upon the assembled company while Jakov examined it gravely, first holding it at arm's length, then close to the tip of his nose.

"*Dobra! Prima!*" he suddenly exclaimed, a huge grin splitting his face in two. That was the signal to announce that we had been accepted, and the thunder of Dalmatian voices broke out on all sides of us. A glass of *Prošek* was pressed into Dick's hand and we were invited to sit on the best chairs. Jakov, meanwhile, roared culinary instructions at Matica that carried clearly above the hubbub in his kitchen.

IN THE VILLAGE OF BRUSJE, HVAR ISLAND, DALMATIA

The Dulčić family with friends and neighbours outside their home in Brusje. Marija, Grandma and Grandpa Dulčić are in the centre, then Luka in the arms of the village schoolmaster and Matica and Jakov Dulčić on the right. March 1969

**CHRISTMAS TIME AT ALL SAINTS ROMAN CATHOLIC SCHOOL
IN MANSFIELD**

Ivana Đerđ - the Christmas angel. (See page 62)

Photo: Courtesy Nottingham Post Group

Jakov, who had been a radio-operator with Tito and Fitzroy Maclean on the Island of Vis in 1944, and Matica, who had also fought with the Partisans, owned a few small vineyards and rosemary and lavender patches on the mountains of Hvar from which they earned their meagre living; and they had a donkey and a mule on which to carry their produce to market.

Several hours after our arrival at Brusje we staggered to our feet, having consumed a four-course luncheon and sampled many glasses of local wine and *rakija* to the accompaniment of some hauntingly beautiful Dalmatian folk-songs. And that was how the seeds of friendship were first sown, which have grown and flourished over the years.

And there were other people on the islands: especially Maté and Vera who ran a *gostionica* (guest house) in the mediaeval village of Splitska on Brač Island. Our second visit to them was an idyllic week in April during which Vera would never allow us to dine elsewhere – always her most special dishes and Maté's best wine for her English guests. When Dick asked for the bill just before we were due to leave, Maté replied, "There is no bill."

Knowing that they had three children and Maté's old mother to support, and he himself was out of work at the time, we protested strongly, but all to no avail. When Dick had finished speaking, Maté rose to his feet and, towering over us with furrowed brows, he repeated; "There is nothing to pay. For us, you must understand, friends are more important than money."

There was no answer to that statement. We went humbly home knowing that we would never forget the Bašković family; and if some chance occurred in the future, we would do everything in our power to repay them.

Vera Basković at her home in Splitska, 1979.

Maté Basković, 1979.

*　　*　　*　　*　　*　　*

During the summer months of 1992 the television news brought us horror after horror from the regions that had been 'ethnically cleansed' in the former Jugoslavia. Thousands of Bosnian refugees joined the hordes of Croatians who had lost their homes during the siege of Vukovar the previous year. Scenes of indescribable misery greeted our eyes, day after day.

Dick and I suddenly knew that we had to DO something to help those wretched homeless people, no matter how small a gesture it might be. It was time to move, instead of sitting around feebly moaning; "How I wish there was something we could do to help ..."

There was an empty flat in the stable block at Thoresby Park, my parents' old home in Nottinghamshire, and it seemed a good starting-point from which to develop our plans. Ken Graham, the Clerk of Works for the past twenty-five years, found us a reliable builder with very few jobs on hand in the middle of the summer holidays. He moved in a few days later, closely followed by a plumber, an electrician and a gang of painters.

The magic transformation of eleven small dark rooms which had been clothed with brownish-green wallpaper, cobwebs and filth took place at lightning speed. By the first week in September it had become a clean bright apartment with white, primrose-yellow and pink as the basic colours in the five bedrooms, two sitting-rooms, dining-room, kitchen and bathrooms. And it was not long before the local people discovered what we were up to and all the generous gifts began to flow in.

Ada Finch, a tiny white-haired lady who resembles a delicate piece of Dresden china, became our greatest ally and hardest task-mistress. Originally District Councillor for the large mining village of Edwinstowe, she strode into battle on the furnishing front before tackling many other vital issues to which we had hardly given a thought. Before many days had passed, rolls of carpet, curtains, armchairs, wardrobes, chests-of-drawers, washing-machines, a cooker ... in fact, every useful household item you could think of arrived in the Stables' courtyard. And, in the middle of all the vans and trucks coming and going, there was the affair of the 3-piece suite.

A family who lived in a bungalow opposite the Finch's home in Edwinstowe had just treated themselves to a new 3-piece suite. On the morning of its delivery they had come to an arrangement with the municipal dust-cart to call round and remove their old one, although it was not dust-bin day till the following Monday. Ada, who was keeping a close surveillance of her neighbour's house from her kitchen window, phoned her friend, Joe Lewis, the moment the old sofa emerged from the back door. Joe arrived with his truck at the same time as the two armchairs joined the sofa. Ada, meanwhile, had sprinted purposefully across the road.

"I noticed your charming new 3-piece suite arriving this morning," she confided to her neighbour with an engaging smile. "What excellent taste you have! Do allow me to be of some small service to you as I happen to have some friends who are desperately trying to furnish an old flat for a group of homeless women and children from Bosnia – you just can't imagine what terrible things those poor creatures have suffered – and I know that my friends would be SO grateful if you could let them have the old set?"

Our good friend, Ada Finch.

"What a brilliant solution! But we have already asked the dust-cart to call around, I'm afraid."

"No problem at all!" Ada bared her small white teeth with satisfaction. "Joe here will take them to Thoresby straight away in his truck, and I'll just give the Cleansing Department a ring. They're all old friends of mine, in any case."

After the dispatch of the 3-piece suite Ada phoned Mr Doxey who was in charge of the remaining furniture at Nottingham General Hospital, which had recently closed down. A few days later Dick and I drove to Nottingham in a large car with a roof-rack, while Malcolm and Cynthia followed in his red truck; Malcolm, a tall strong man with a beguilingly gentle expression on his face, used to be Head Gardener at Thoresby during my mother's lifetime. When he heard that Dick and I were planning to build a comparatively small house in a walled field full of giant weeds, he announced that he was going to become our gardener – which he has been for the last seven years.

We were received by a charming and helpful Mr Doxey – what on earth had Ada said to him, I wondered? And a few hours later we left Nottingham with as many beds, small chests-of-drawers and bedside cabinets as we could fit into the two vehicles.

During that rumbustious period of preparation, the people nearer home, those who lived in the villages of Perlethorpe and Budby, were far from idle. There were only a few rumblings in the undergrowth, a typical one coming from an old pensioner who also lived in a flat above the stables. He had come to England as a refugee from Latvia during the Second

Cynthia and Malcolm at our 25th wedding anniversary.

World War and worked in Sherwood Forest for many years, until his retirement.

"Ve don't vant any bluedee furrenners round here!" he was rumoured to have said in his thick Baltic accent. "Send 'em all back vere they belongs."

A large room in the same building was used by Edgar Liepins as his workshop. He was also a native of the Baltic countries, but his approach to the imminent arrival of the refugees was quite different. Edgar and his wife, Barbara, gave us a double bed, three single beds, a wardrobe, two armchairs and an oak table which he took infinite trouble in repolishing, as well as a bedspread, bath-towels and a large rug.

There were so many wonderful people who arrived bearing gifts during those hectic days in September. The workmen had almost finished their jobs, and some of us had begun the arduous task of furnishing the flat and transforming it into a real home.

The Agent of the Thoresby Estates, Rowan McFerran, returned from his holiday about that time. He is a man of power and consequence, Mr BIG on the estates, and he was not at all pleased when he perceived the beelike activity which had been taking place without his knowledge in the old stables.

"I DID try to phone you in Norfolk but couldn't find your number," I lied unconvincingly. "And the builders just happened to have a free slot to fit us in, while everyone was away on holiday."

He is also a man of considerable charm and tact, so he took it well after the first shock waves had subsided; but I can well imagine what he must have said about us once we were out of earshot! He was, however, just in time to point out some serious defects like the absence of a proper fire escape, and the possible breakdown of the electricity supply to all the houses in the stables complex if we put too many electrical gadgets into the flat.

Rowan and Janet McFerran at the entrance to the old stables at Thoresby.

I mentioned before that some of us had begun the task of turning the big empty flat into a home. But it was Cynthia, in the role of Commander-in-Chief, and her husband, Malcolm, who undertook the bulk of the work while the rest of us hovered around the edges, obeying Cynthia's crisp commands and helping wherever we could.

Cynthia is tall and handsome with coal-black hair, luminous brown eyes and a straight look that can reduce lesser mortals to gibbering idiots when required. Eleven rooms and a long corridor and staircase leading up to it is a lot of floor space to cover; but she and Malcolm cut, hammered and stamped the carpets into position for twelve long days, and half the nights as well, until the bare paint-stained floors glowed with blue, green, red, brown and yellow pile. Snatches of song drifted through the windows on the north side of the old stable block, and people began to call regularly "to have a quick butchers", as one couple put it.

Ada and Wilf Finch came nearly every day, usually laden with bags of clothing, more furniture, kitchen utensils, and all kinds of useful things for the setting up of a new home. Malcolm drew up in his red truck one morning with the back filled with dolls, Teddy Bears and woolly toys sent by his sister for the children we hoped to have.

Rowan looked in most days to see what fresh horrors we were perpetrating and to keep an eye on our progress. And Mrs Chicken, who ran the Perlethorpe Social Club, arrived with a trunk full of curtains, blankets, cushion covers and clothes. She had organized a raffle at the club to raise £50 to help stock the larder before the refugees arrived. Then there was Peter Leplar from the local Rotary Club who turned up when we were having our tea-break one morning. He returned a few days later with Alan Wood, the Chairman of the Nottinghamshire Rotary Club. I remember saying to Cynthia at the time, "Why do we have to suffer from all these busy-bodies who just come here to waste our time?"

But it was not until weeks later that we fully appreciated how much those two men and some of their friends in the Rotary Club were doing to help our four families, and to bring some sunshine into their lives during the early days.

Cynthia was sitting behind her sewing-machine in the kitchen by the beginning of October, cutting and hemming endless pairs of curtains to fit all the windows. Malcolm and Dick, meanwhile, and one or two other strong men who volunteered for work, were busy carrying heavy pieces of furniture up the stairs and into the flat.

"Wouldn't that wardrobe look just perfect in the pink bedroom down the far end of the passage?" I suggested to Cynthia; the men, with heavy sighs and ferocious grunts to keep us aware of their valiant efforts, had just deposited it in Bedroom Number 1 at the other end of the flat.

"Yes, that's just where I had planned to put it myself!" Cynthia confided to me, one eyelid behaving like the shutter on a camera while the men cursed us under their breath as they set off down the long corridor.

Dick's worst task of all, he revealed later, was taking some of the heavy Victorian doors off their hinges and sawing slices of wood off their bottoms so that when they were back on their hinges they would be able to close over the thick carpets which covered some of the floors.

Elizabeth Roberson from Budby came every day to polish and dust all the furniture as it moved in, and to make up the beds and vacuum the carpets. Then there was Connie Bollans and Elizabeth Williams, the Vicar's wife, who spent many hours sorting through the mass of secondhand clothing that arrived in black plastic bags from all over Nottinghamshire. My job during that period was to hang pictures –

Mother's old watercolour and oil landscapes, especially her Jugoslav paintings – three per room, several in the long corridor and a few rather special ones in the big sitting-room.

We made a point of having frequent tea-breaks – invariably cheerful gatherings when the workers and those who had merely come to have a butchers and offer advice sat around the kitchen shouting merrily at one another. I remember thinking on more than one occasion that this was rather a happy period – a sort of lively overture before the grand opera began in earnest. No one knew what kind of people would be living in those rooms, nor whether we would like them and they would grow to like us in time? I often tried to picture them and how they would feel about their new home; especially after we had placed all the big pieces of furniture and started allotting the ornaments, pictures and toys to each room.

Ken Graham used to look in most days to see how we were getting along, and one morning he turned up with two lovely pieces of furniture – a glass-fronted cabinet and a matching sideboard in polished satin-wood. They added the final touch of class to the big sitting-room.

"When we've finished all this we'll have a party for everyone concerned – a special celebration," I announced, visualizing a dozen or so people who had given most generously and helped in so many ways.

The party finally took place some four months later, and there were more than a hundred people to invite by then!

Chapter 2 - Obstacles

The furnishing of the flat in the old stables at Thoresby was well under way before one of our visitors let drop a few discreet inquiries about the date when the refugees were expected to arrive.

This was a sore subject as far as Dick and I were concerned, a question to which we had no immediate answer. Ever since we had first conceived the idea back in that June of 1992, long before the builders moved into the flat, we had announced to all and sundry that we were planning to drive out to Croatia in October in a couple of mini-buses, and bring home with us eight or ten refugees. The mini-buses had been offered free by a firm in East Anglia, two old friends, an experienced driver and a nurse, had volunteered to come with us and, to begin with, we perceived no particular obstacles to our plan.

I telephoned one or two people who had made similar journeys during the summer, and returned safely with their cargoes of refugees to face the television cameras on arrival in Dover – and considerable applause from their fellow-countrymen. That was when the first doubts began to creep in.

None of those heroes were prepared to reveal exactly where they had been to secure their refugees and, long afterwards, we discovered that some of them were receiving large sums of money from well-endowed immigrants from Croatia, who were driving their limousines to the Austrian frontier with Slovenia to meet their benefactors!

Those were certainly not the type of refugees we were anxious to help. It was the ordinary people from small homes who had been 'ethnically cleansed' and lost everything, for whom we were searching and, according to the newspapers, there were a good few thousand of them languishing in makeshift summer camps. Our friend, Jean Melhuish, the nurse who had volunteered to come with us, had long-standing connections with the Kentish Red Cross and asked them for the address of the Head Person in London.

"That's a brilliant idea," I told her. "They're doing so much good work out in Bosnia that they're sure to know of hundreds of refugees who'd like to come to England."

Well, I wrote to Mr Ernest Stevens at the Red Cross Headquarters in Grosvenor Crescent, and several weeks later received a very stuffy reply. After a few polite opening remarks he informed me that "the British Red Cross is not involved in arranging the evacuation of adults and children from the former Jugoslavia. This is the policy taken with careful regard to the current situation and the policy and experience of the International Committee of the Red Cross and the United Nations High Commissioner for Refugees, leading agencies in the conflict area.

We would advise anyone contemplating arranging for an 'unofficial' evacuation of people to the U.K. to contact their local Social Services Department and Department of Health, so that they can inform you of the immediate difficulties and the broader implications of such an action.

Thank you for your concern.

> Yours sincerely,
> Ernest Stevens
> (International Welfare Department)"

So that was that! We then wrote to Michael Nicholson, c/o Independent Television News, as he had just rescued a little girl from a refugee camp for orphans in Bosnia; but there was no reply, and some months later the letter was returned to us marked "Gone away".

Dick and I finally decided that the only way to tackle the problem was to drive out to Croatia as soon as the flat was ready, and go to a refugee camp to see if we could find two families who would like to come back with us to England. It seemed a simple enough plan, but we soon began to worry about how we should manage to cross the various frontiers with a group of people without passports, and whether we would be allowed to bring them into England at the end of the journey.

Early in October we had a telephone conversation with an army doctor out in Zagreb. She was the daughter of one of Dick's oldest friends and she had spent the past few months working in the hospital in Sarajevo. She was due to return to England in a few days' time but, before her departure, she put us in touch with Lars Nielsen, the U.N. High Commissioner for Refugees in Zagreb. Dick spoke to him on the telephone on two occasions and we began to feel that we were at last getting somewhere. He was a nice man who did not place countless obstacles in our way; and he confirmed that he could find us several thousand families who would love the chance of coming to England! But, despite our renewed optimism, there was still one serious problem that we had to deal with ourselves before coming to fetch them; and he detailed what was required in a fax he sent to Dick on October 14th –

"Dear Dr Raynes,

This is to acknowledge reception of your facsimile message of 2 & 7 October regarding accommodation for two ex-Jugoslav refugee families in Nottinghamshire, U.K.

The now most needy refugees in ex-Jugoslavia are those being expelled from Bosnia and Hercegovina, mainly ethnic Muslims, but also ethnic Croats without Croatian citizenship and Serbs of mixed marriages. They are generally not admitted into Croatia, or they are admitted only to be returned to other parts of Bosnia and Hercegovina and – in most cases – drafted (i.e. for military service).

Even though U.K. Immigration does not require visas for citizens of ex-Jugoslavia, there are still some concerns related to the realization of your proposal:

a) The persons in question must carry valid passports to get admission on regular tourist terms to U.K.

b) If the persons in question are draftable, i.e. males 16-60 years, females 19-55 years, if not mothers to minor children; a permission to leave must be obtained by the Bosnia-Hercegovinian representatives in Zagreb.

c) A written declaration to confirm further travel and final entry to the U.K. for the persons in question will be necessary to grant exit/ transit to/ through Slovenia and maybe other countries, given that transportation goes over land.

I realize it may all sound a bit discouraging, yet our intention is only to avoid to the extent possible the risk of a forced return to conflict areas and a forced division of families.

For further advice and detailed information regarding formalities etc., you are welcome to approach our London office, who will be notified with a copy of this message. The address is:

UNHCR, 7, Westminster Palace Gardens, Artillery Row,
9B – LONDON – SW1P 1RL.

Finally, allow me to express on behalf of the refugees in ex-Jugoslavia my gratitude for your concern and efforts.

Best regards,
Lars Lynge Nielsen
FIELD COORDINATOR"

"Well, that sounds quite hopeful," Dick ventured. "All we have to do now is to get a written agreement from the Head of Immigration in Dover, saying that he will let us all in when we return there."

My thoughts immediately turned to Jack Dawson, Commodore of Townsend Ferries, who used to be my Captain when I worked as a purser on the cross-Channel run. Although he had been retired for some years, he still had many friends and contacts in the shipping and immigration world and would, I felt sure, be able to put us in touch with the right man to solve our problem.

A few days later Dick and I found ourselves preparing tea aboard our sailing-boat, *ROSKILDE,* for a Mr and Mrs Cyril Allen who lived at Kirby-le-Soken, Essex. He was a keen yachtsman who kept his boat in the same marina as ours, and he was also an old friend of Jack Dawson's and had been the Head of Customs and Immigration in Dover for many years during the time that Jack was Senior Master of the Townsend Ferries. Jack had already explained our needs to him over the telephone before we met, and he had been in touch with the Home Office and the current Immigration Chief at Dover on our behalf.

The Allens were a charming couple and we spent several hours chatting with them in *ROSKILDE's* cabin; but the outcome of that meeting placed us no nearer to our goal than when we started. The Dover Customs, as we were well aware, had already allowed a number of coaches filled with refugees to pass through – all those lucky operators with high profiles of whom we had read in the newspapers and seen on television news. Mr Allen declared that it was extremely unlikely that anyone would be turned back on arrival at Dover.

But – the big and all-important BUT – his colleagues refused to sign any documents (even if they contained every known detail about the refugees concerned) stating that they would definitely allow them to enter this country, as it was against official government policy to let any more homeless people from the former Jugoslavia come to England.

"Stalemate once again!" we groaned, after the Allens had left us. "I wonder what Lars Nielsen is going to say to that."

What he did say, the following day, was not encouraging. Since Dick had last spoken to him there had been a new twist to the business of exporting refugees to other parts of Europe. A group had been turned back at the frontier of the country to which they were bound, and when they finally returned to Croatia, they were refused re-entry into their own country.

"On no account must we allow this to happen again." Lars stressed each word. "Those poor tragic women and children 'floating' in a hostile world with nowhere to lay their heads. So, I am very sorry to tell you, Dr Raynes, but I will not release to you any of our families unless you can bring written proof of their acceptance by your government."

*　　*　　*　　*　　*　　*

We drove back to Nottinghamshire next day. It was already the third week in October, and a few menacing whispers reached us about the impending removal of some of the furniture if no refugees showed up very soon! Then Ada phoned to say that one old lady was furious because she had not yet received a "thank-you" letter for the contents of her black dustbin-liner.

I had already written no less than seventy-five "thank-you" letters, and when I asked about what had emerged from that particular bag, I learnt that it was a rather grubby pair of ancient corsets and two frayed brassiéres!

Cynthia arrived with a gleam in her eyes next morning. "Have you had a look at the Mansfield Chad yet?" she asked. "I left it on the kitchen table for you to see."

"No, not yet," I admitted. "I was far too busy writing ten more "thank-you" letters last night to read anything at all."

"Well, there a picture of a Mansfield coach-driver in it, and he's just come home with a coach-load of refugees from Jugoslavia; and, what's more, he says he's going there again very soon, before the winter sets in, to bring back another lot."

"Lucky man!" Dick sighed; "He must have some special friends in the Dover Immigration Department, I suppose."

"Still, it's worth giving him a ring just in case he could give us a few tips," I suggested.

"You remember what happened with all the others we've tackled in the past three months?" my husband muttered pessimistically. "But you can try if you like, and good luck to you!"

I seized the telephone and, glory be to God, the man himself picked up the receiver at the other end of the line. His name was Mick Gelsthorpe and it appeared that he ran a small coach company called Janick Travel from his home in Mansfield. He was not at all averse to telling me about his past experiences in the former Jugoslavia, nor his plans for the next trip out there for which he was busy collecting money at that time.

"I tell you what, I was planning to come over to Ollerton this afternoon on a spot of business anyway so I might as well pop in to see you while I'm in the neighbourhood, if that suits you?"

It suited us very well, and a few hours later Mick was ensconced in a large armchair in our study, describing some of the tragic scenes he had come across during his last journey through Slovenia and Croatia. He was a big man with dark hair and a moustache to match, and his eyes looked moist behind the tinted glass in his spectacles as he told us about a little half-starved boy to whom he had given a bar of chocolate on the roadside in Croatia, which had been received with intense joy.

"I'll never forget the look on that kiddie's face," Mick declared. "And it's for the likes of him and all the other thousands what've lost their homes, that I'll keep trying to rescue as many as possible."

He was hoping to bring back at least thirty-five mothers and children on his next run the following week, and was delighted to hear that we would be prepared to offer a home to eight, or perhaps ten people, on his return. Despite the gruesome scenes on television news every night, it was becoming increasingly hard to find suitable homes for the refugees, Mick told us, and the local Social Services were not being particularly helpful.

"Can we come with you on the coach?" I pleaded. "Dick is a doctor and I can speak Serbo-Croat, so you might find us quite useful."

"Sorry, Loov, but we're full up already," Mick spread out his hands. "There's that many volunteers wants to coom for the ride, and if we don't watch out there'll be no room left for the poor refugees, see what I mean?"

We saw what he meant quite clearly, so had to compromise by saying that we would try to organize a special reception party for them when they first landed at Dover, and we would be there ourselves to welcome them as long as they arrived before November 7th, when we had to be back at Thoresby without fail.

"We reckon to be back at least a week before then," Mick assured us; "and it's a big weight off my mind to have found such a loovely home for two of my families. I was getting dead woorried about where to find homes for them all."

Mick drove away into the autumn dusk while Dick and I stood in the road inhaling the sweet smell of wood-smoke rising from the chimneys of Meadow Cottages.

"I believe that man may be the answer to our prayers," I murmured to Dick. "Even if we can't go out there to fetch them ourselves, he seems to understand what we are trying to do, and to have the same feelings as us about whom to bring home!"

"Well, at least we shall be able to look people in the eyes again round here, especially the old buzzards who are threatening to remove their furniture!" Dick grinned cheerfully as we turned to go back indoors.

Chapter 3 - The Journey's End

The old stables at Thoresby were built around a large and elegant courtyard during the Victorian era. The approach road passes through a splendid archway surmounted by a pair of stone turrets, and there is room to house at least twenty horses and numerous carriages, with the grooms' quarters on the floors above. The buildings are surrounded by beautiful parkland and deer pasture, and a fleeting glimpse through the trees gives a surprising vision of a fortified Norman farmhouse which has been miraculously transported into the heart of Sherwood Forest.

The Old Stables at Thoresby Park with the windows of the Croatian's flat on the first floor. Photo: Courtesy of Newark Advertiser

There are no horses living there today, and the west side of the stable block has been converted into an art gallery. My mother's paintings form a permanent exhibition at one end, and modern artists rent the other half of the gallery for their own exhibitions. Then there is the restaurant run by Bill and Beryl Blagg, and several coach-houses filled with old furniture, two sailing-dinghies, an ancient fire engine and ladder for rescuing people from high up, fourteen bicycles and the newest arrivals – a pair of black and white rabbits.

John the Bee, as he is known locally, lives on the first floor of the north block – it was he who was reputed to have stressed that he did not wish to see any more "bluedee furrenners" round there. And just across the passage from John's place is situated the refugees' flat.

It was like a beehive in full buzz during the first week in November. Cynthia, the Queen Bee, was enthroned behind her sewing-machine in the kitchen – very much in charge of the entire stable block – while a stream of kind-hearted people bearing gifts climbed the stone staircase up to the flat and received brisk instructions about how to make themselves useful on arrival. The larder was quickly transformed from a bleak little room lined with empty shelves into an Aladdin's cave filled with tea, coffee, sugar, tinned food, cakes, biscuits, flour, yeast, cooking oil, herbs and a hundred other useful things with which to feed our unknown guests. The bathroom and shower-room over-flowed with soap, hair shampoos, dusting-powder, rolls of lavatory paper and Lux soap flakes. Mick Gelsthorpe sent round a washing-machine which had been given him as a result of his appeal in the Mansfield Chad. Dick and I, meanwhile, purchased a deep-freeze, and various friends soon appeared with legs of lamb, joints of beef, chickens, fish and a selection of vegetables to help fill the freezer.

We were not sure whether our refugees would turn out to be Muslims from Bosnia or Croats from the early part of the war around Vukovar and Krajina, so we decided to play safe and not buy them any pork, ham or bacon. The final touch was a broad band of white cloth stretched across the entrance archway on the north side of the stable-yard. Rowan McFerran's son, Jack, had painted across it in large red letters the words *"DOBRO DOŠLI"* – which means "WELCOME" in Serbo-Croat.

*   *   *   *   *   *

The two coaches from Janick Travel left England at the end of October and motored almost non-stop to Slovenia. They paused there to drop a load of medicines, warm blankets and winter clothing at one of the big refugee camps, before driving across the mountains into Croatia to pick up their passengers for the return journey.

"It's all sorted out," Mick told us before they left. "We've a contact in Rijeka who'll have seen to all the paper-work before we get there, and have our moothers and kiddies all together and ready to leave. We should be home within five or six days if everything goars according to plan."

A lady we knew as 'Rosemary' from Mansfield, was acting as co-ordinator between Mick Gelsthorpe and all those interested in his return to Nottinghamshire. She was a marvellous person – concise, dependable, unruffled, and always cheerful and polite, even if you were the five hundredth call she had received during the past twelve hours. She had a friend, Bobby, who had gone as a nurse to the expedition, and it was she who phoned home every evening and gave Rosemary a clear picture of what was going on at the Croatian end of the line – the unforeseen happenings which were to cause a serious disruption to their plans.

It appeared that the two coaches arrived on time at Rijeka, the big seaport at the northern end of the archipelago that stretches for two hundred miles along the coast of the former Jugoslavia. The drivers, interpreters, nurses and other helpers emerged from their coaches, very tired but satisfied with their progress. It was then that the bombshell exploded! Their all-important reliable contact, who was to have completed all the arrangements for them, had disappeared without a trace.

"He just did a runner!" Bobby explained to her friend in Mansfield; "So here we are with nothing ready, no refugees waiting to come to England, and our money will soon run out I shouldn't wonder, as one of our interpreters booked us all into a posh hotel in Opatija, which is a smart seaside place a few miles from Rijeka."

*   *   *   *   *   *

Jean Melhuish, meanwhile, had gathered together a group of dedicated friends at St Margaret's Bay, near Dover, who had volunteered to prepare a nourishing meal for the two coach parties in the village hall soon after their arrival in England. Dick and I travelled south to be ready to receive Mick and the refugees in Dover, but the actual time of the ferry they would be able to catch from Calais had been left vague; we were, however, all expecting the great arrival to take place sometime on November 4th.

Well, we waited and waited, and the ladies of St Margaret's Bay preserved an amazing aura of calmness in the face of constantly changing news bulletins regarding the whereabouts of our refugees. We were in hourly touch with Rosemary who related to us the latest tidings from Croatia.

"One of the interpreters who travelled out from England with our party has been searching the camps round Rijeka for the past two days," she reported; "and she's managed to collect a group of thirty-seven mothers and children who want to come to England. Some of them have been refugees since the fall of Vukovar in 1991, and others were burnt out of their homes when the Serbs invaded Krajina. She found one family living in a dark underground garage, and another young pregnant mother who had walked a hundred miles over the mountains leading a boy of two by the hand, to reach comparative safety."

The other helpers from England, meanwhile, who were installed in the best hotel in Opatija, had misunderstood the price of their rooms when they called at the reception desk on their arrival. They discovered to their horror on the third day that the rooms and meals were twice as much as they had calculated, and there would hardly be enough money in the kitty to pay their bill!

Mick promptly announced that they must leave at once. As there was no time to cope with all the official paper-work, he prepared a large document himself on which he inscribed the names, dates of birth and places of origin of his refugee passengers; and he promised anyone who showed an interest in their welfare that he would bring them back to Croatia in six months' time.

John Abbott, a very large and occasionally fierce-looking driver from Mansfield, proved to be a tower of strength in rounding up the refugees, calming their fears about the future and striking up a bond of friendship with the children.

"John is quite superb!" Rosemary told me. "He has no fear of anyone who starts using threatening behaviour – he had plenty of that to deal with at the camp in Ljubljana where they dropped off their cargo on the way down. And he's marvellous at cheering up the mothers when they're feeling very sad, and keeping the kids happy on the long journey across Europe."

Two days later we had a phone call from Mick himself to say that they had just crossed the German frontier and were heading north at full speed. Some of the host families back in England were proving difficult, he confided, and as he did not want to split up any of the refugees' family groups, would we mind taking fourteen – four mothers and ten children – instead of the ten we had agreed to before he left?

"Well ... we'll have to give it some serious thought," Dick hedged. "We'll discuss it with you when you reach Mansfield."

We had been unable to wait around any longer at St Margaret's Bay as it was the day before the Annual Tenant's Dinner at Thoresby, an occasion which we could not miss. Jean, however, had at last received from Rosemary a definite day and time when the coaches were due to reach Dover, so she and her team of helpers were able to start their preparations in the village hall.

*   *   *   *   *   *

John Gradiški, a Croat married to an Englishwoman who had lived near Mansfield for many years, was one of the interpreters who accompanied Mick Gelsthorpe on his journey. The coaches were met outside the Dover custom-house by Jack Dawson, my former Captain, and Jill Blowers, another good friend of ours from St Margaret's Bay. Jack led the way in his car to the village, where the exhausted travellers climbed our of their coaches in the car-park near the old Norman church.

The refugees climbing down from their coach to be welcomed by Jean Melhuish at St Margaret's Bay. Photo: Courtesy of Kent Messenger Group.

"There were tears pouring down my face when I saw those smiling welcoming faces," John Gradiški told me later. "We had been traversing Europe for two days and nights with hardly a stop and many of our people were sad to leave their husbands and old parents behind, as well as being frightened about the future – you see, they'd never left their own country

Chicken soup being served by Eileen Barber to Marjan and Josip Hržić.
Photo: Courtesy of Kent Messenger Group

before and did not know what to expect. And suddenly we were all sitting down eating a wonderful thick chicken soup, followed by apple pie and big mugs of sweet tea, with so many friendly people fussing around us. Then there was the wash place, with a clean new shirt for everyone to change into; and, can you picture it, those angels had collected together seventy-six cuddly toys, so there were two each for all our children and a few more besides.

"We were not allowed to stay there for long as Mick wanted to get home to Mansfield that night, but I shall never forget the welcome they gave us ... not as long as I live."

John Gradiški, of course, had only been out of England, his adopted country, for about eight days; but each person on those two coaches viewed their arrival through a different pair of eyes. Katica (the mother who shared with us her bottle of *šljivovic*) had a fourteen-year-old daughter, Natali, and a few months later she wrote down for me her impressions of the last part of their journey to England:

"I sit in the coach and look at the big ship that floats on the blue sea. We shall go aboard that big ship at any moment and begin our journey – the journey which will lead us to our new home.

"I never liked ships and I was very frightened, not only of the sea but the journey we were about to undertake. A thousand questions passed through my mind: Would it be nice when we arrive there? How would my new school be? In a short while would we be able to forget the fear we have experienced? And many more questions for which I was not able to find an answer.

"After several minutes we went on board the ship. I installed myself beside the window and stared into infinity. All I could see in the distance was a line which joined the earth to the sky. It appeared that we would never leave that blue surface of the sea. When I turned away for a moment, however, it awoke my fear more than ever.

"And in this way arrived the moment when everyone was saying, "That is England!" But I saw nothing but huge rocks.

"Out-of-doors there was a thick fog, and in front of my eyes arose one enormous hill, without trees, on which I could distinguish no trace of life; all was divided, like in a wilderness. In that moment I longed to return home, but it was too late. It was not until several hours later that I realized it had only been an ugly fantasy.

"Through the coach windows I saw beautiful green fields, lambs squeaking and skipping like children; it was all like a fairy-tale, but it was real. When we finally came to the house where we would sleep that night, I began to cry. Everyone spoke a strange language and I felt deep grief from the heart, thinking of Daddy and my friends and looking back on my life. I comprehended that I was no longer a child, and I must bravely stride forward into the future and prepare myself for good or evil.

"In the morning we collected together our things, and had only to wait for the people with whom we would go. And in the evening we came to our NEW HOME. Each person was allotted their room, and we all collapsed for a long night's sleep.

"When I went out in the morning I could hardly believe it ... all was wonderful, forest, the trees, marvellously natural – just like a dream! I had always wished to awake in such a place, but I found it hard to believe that what I had wished would not be refused. Perhaps my wish had been realized after all?

"I and my family felt as if we were at home, and I am able to say to you from my heart; "Thank you, *Gospodin* Dick and *Gospodja* Rozelle, and all the people here who wished us welcome and who made it feel like home.

"My heart is still in Croatia, with the children who are hungry and dying this winter, because I know that if I had not come to England I would be one of them."

Chapter 4 - The New Home

We said "Yes", of course, to making a home for fourteen refugees – especially after our first meeting with them at Skegby Hall, the Social Services reception centre, the morning after their arrival in Mansfield. But even before reaching that decision, four more beds had mysteriously found their way across the stable-yard and crept up the stairs into the flat – almost, it seemed, of their own free will!

Skegby Hall was a daunting, heaving mass of social workers, vicars, would-be hosts and hostesses, doctors, nurses and reporters, with the thirty-seven mothers and children wandering through the stark, no-nonsense rooms like sheep which had strayed into some alien pasture. Everyone was expected to have a medical examination but, as very few of the Croatians spoke English, they were spared the traumas of listening to the plans for their future health-care. Some of the mothers stared, unseeing, into the busy ants' hill around them recalling, perhaps, the country they had so recently left and wondering miserably if they would ever see home again. A few of the children, on the other hand, were treating the whole affair as a great adventure, their eyes bright and shiny and their knowledge of English (learnt at school in Croatia) being proudly displayed. There were no Bosnian Muslims amongst them – they were all Catholics who had lost their homes in 1991.

Dick and I were introduced to Rosemary – our telephone friend – and Bobby, the nurse; and they, in turn, introduced us to some of the mothers and children who were destined to become OUR families.

Anica Hržić, described by Bobby as "the conscience of the whole group – she was always trying to stop us sharing our sweets or spending our money on them," was the first mother I remembered meeting. Quite small, with smooth dark hair and emotional brown eyes, she had a rather beautiful face and was wearing a long black coat over an emerald-green woollen dress which looked surprisingly elegant, when one reflected that it was, perhaps, her only outfit, apart from a jersey and some jeans.

"*Dobro jutro!* (Good morning!)," I ventured in my best Croatian. "*Milo mi je da Vas vidim* (I am very pleased to meet you)."

Anica smiled broadly and told me that I spoke very good Croatian, but soon perceived that she must speak slowly and distinctly to make me understand. In that way we found that we could communicate quite easily with one another, and Anica would often act as spokeswoman for the whole group when there were any *problemas* to discuss. She had three children: Antonija, aged fourteen, who had a thick crop of brownish-gold hair, like Alice in Wonderland, and the most amazing straight dark eyebrows; her brother, Marjan, a year younger, with a handsome but rather remote face; and little Josip, aged eleven, who had big rabbit teeth and a joyful personality which was to gain him many friends.

We had not been talking for many minutes before Anica beckoned to her cousin, Marica Đerđ, as she and her three children were also coming to live at Thoresby. Both families came from Ilok, a small town near Vukovar which was among the first places to be 'ethnically cleansed' by the Serbs in October 1991.

Marica was a very nice person who emitted waves of warmth and sunshine whenever she smiled. A few years older than Anica, she had a birthmark in the shape of a large pimple on her right eyelid close to the bridge of her nose, which the nurses and social workers pounced on at once.

"We must get that fixed as soon as she's settled," they announced; "a small operation and we'll soon see the last of that hideous thing!"

Marica, although she understood no English, sensed that they were talking about her and looked at us apprehensively. We swiftly changed the subject by asking to meet her children.

Marijana, her eighteen-year-old daughter, was a tall girl with long brown hair, a gentle expression and the same sunny smile as her mother. She came to meet us with her little sister, Ivana, the only blonde with blue eyes among the refugees, who had the face of a rather wistful angel. I noticed that the reporters and photographers who had crowded into Skegby Hall were drawn towards her as if by a magnet, and I remember wondering if she was as nice as she looked and if all that attention would spoil her.

Marica's youngest child was a boy of six called Damir. He had dark hair and luminous brown eyes, and the mischievous expression of a baby chimpanzee.

The group around us had grown quite large when a teenage girl with a powerful presence pushed her way through the crowd and, holding out her right hand, declared in excellent English, "I am Dragana and I come to live with you also!"

Dragana Franjković was an intelligent and serious-minded girl who was to worry a great deal about her education and her future in the months ahead. She soon became our most accomplished interpreter, and her best friend turned out to be Katica's daughter, Natali, which was one reason why those two families did not wish to be separated. But we had no chance to meet her mother and brother, nor Katica's family, on that occasion as a bell rang peremptorily to announce lunch-time at Skegby Hall. We hastily took our leave and were told to expect our contingent of refugees – Mick would drive them over himself – in the late afternoon.

*   *   *   *   *   *

Back at Thoresby, the Trustees' luncheon-party was in full swing in the Pierrepont Gallery on the west side of the stable-yard. It was quite a contrast to the rumbustious beehive of Skegby Hall – an annual gathering of Trustees, Estate Agents and their wives and cousins of mine with their families – a serious get-together to discuss estate business, the influence of the EEC on farming, the price of timber, pheasant and partridge shooting and the problems of some of the pensioners. But my oldest cousin, Elizabeth Grant, the widow of the man who had steered Thoresby successfully through three decades of financial hazards, was hardly listening to the conversation batting to and fro around her. Her eyes, as bright as winter stars, were focussed on the windows in front of her, and she sometimes paused with a forkload of roast pheasant half way to her mouth to exclaim; "I wonder how soon they'll turn up? D'you think they'll get here before we have to leave?"

Elizabeth had already been on a conducted tour of the flat and noticed the fresh flowers arranged in vases in most of the rooms, the coal fires burning merrily behind their highly-polished grates and the big open trunk in the sitting-room, filled to overflowing with a marvellous selection of toys given us by Malcolm's sister. There were Teddy Bears dressed in multi-coloured pyjamas, woolly lambs, rabbits and ducks, and dolls wearing pink and blue dresses with bonnets to match. The final touches were being added by Malcolm and Cynthia, as well as Ada Finch who had come over after morning church to organize a sumptuous meal for fourteen people.

"You leave all that to me and I'll make sure they have a really nice meat dinner soon after they get here. You've got enough on your hands as it is," Ada informed me the previous week.

She had already been in touch with Social Services about the rights of refugees to claim a small weekly allowance, the questions of health care, schooling, heating, etc; and she had persuaded the National Coal Board to come to Thoresby the day after their arrival, to bring them a free gift of coal to last the whole winter. I sometimes wondered how we would have managed without Ada and the way she overcame the biggest problems with her charming smile and will of iron, and all her friends in the corridors of power.

Carolin, Elizabeth's daughter, dragged her mother away very reluctantly about four o'clock, as they had a long journey home across the Pennines to Shropshire. All our other luncheon guests left in small groups, and the dark descended on the stable-yard like a damp grey blanket.

"What a pity they didn't arrive before sunset," I complained to Dick. "They may get lost trying to find their way here in the dark, and they won't be able to see the "Welcome" sign over the door nor what a lovely ..."

A pair of headlights appeared at that moment under the archway, and a large coach crept slowly into the stable-yard.

"Here they come at last!" Ada called to us from an upstairs window. "Better put my saucepans back on the stove."

Dick and I waited impatiently for the coach door to open. The great moment had come at last, after the endless weeks of striving, planning and disappointments.

"It looks to me as if there are far more than fourteen people and a driver inside that coach," I whispered to him. "I wonder who they all are?"

The coach doors suddenly opened and a swarm of people with Nottinghamshire accents whom I did not recognize sprang out into the courtyard. There were some small children with them who shouted excitedly as they thrust us aside and raced through the entrance to the flats without pausing for a moment to notice *"Dobro Došli"* written above them.

"Where are our four families?" I asked Mick, who was just leaving his seat. "I haven't seen a single person I recognize so far, apart from you!"

"Oh, they'll be soomwhere at back end of coach," he told me. "I dare say t'oothers want to have a look round first."

Dick and I turned and sped back up the stairs of the flat to see what was going on up there. This was not at all how we had planned it. There were people in every room, all the way along the corridor: social workers, coach-drivers and their families, interpreters and general hangers-on. Somehow they had stormed the entrance and pushed their way past Cynthia and Ada – no easy feat – then spread out like an oil slick that will seep into every nook and cranny.

I raced along to Bedroom No. 1, but the two women in there were admiring Mother's watercolours so I paused to tell them where she had painted them. By the time I reached the kitchen Anica and her children had managed to fight their way through the front door, so I was able to welcome them to their new home.

"Divno! Krasno!" she exclaimed, spreading out her hands to encompass what she had seen so far.

"Come and see the big sitting-room," I proposed in my best Croatian. "I hope you will find that even more *"Krasno* (beautiful)."

Nearly everyone else had crowded in there by that time, so Anica and I had to force our way into the room, closely followed by her three children. I was just about to point out the special surprise awaiting them – the trunk full of toys – when a wave of anger swept over me, leaving me almost speechless! For there were the terrible shrieking English brats grabbing at the toys and chucking them all over the floor so that hardly a single one remained inside the trunk; and all the pretty dolls' dresses and woolly pyjamas made for the bears were being torn to pieces by those mean youngsters, before our refugee children had even seen them.

Cynthia and I stepped into battle and threw the monsters out of the sitting-room, whereupon they created havoc in the nearest bedroom instead. It appeared that they were the offspring of a coach-driver whose young wife had been one of the party who went to Croatia. Neither she nor her husband made the slightest attempt to control their children and teach them good manners, which was in sharp contrast to the Croatians and made us feel quite ashamed of our fellow-countrymen.

There was, however, one man in the party from Mansfield who seemed different from all his companions: a large powerful man wearing a black knitted cap and thick jersey, he had a rough unshaven face and a shy manner that endeared him to us straight away. I noticed that all OUR children, who had at last found their way into the flat, seemed to be on very friendly terms with him, and his eyes lit up with pleasure whenever one of them approached him. It was not until much later that we discovered he was 'Big John', the man whom Rosemary had described so vividly on the telephone.

The last mother to enter the sitting-room was Janja Franjković, a tall striking lady with jet black hair and a straight look that could pierce any veils of deception in a matter of seconds.

"My god, she looks just like Cynthia's twin sister!" Dick and I exclaimed simultaneously.

Janja was the mother of Dragana, the serious teenager who had spoken such good English when we met her that morning at Skegby Hall. She also had a nine-year-old son called Dragan. She and Katica appeared to be good friends, and their daughters, Natáli and Dragana, were clearly inseparable. Janja's family came from Krajina, the area which was 'ethnically cleansed' by the Serbs during the summer of 1991.

There were about thirty people clustered around the fireplace in the big sitting-room when Katica appeared, clasping her precious bottle of *šljivovic*. Excluding the children, for whom we provided Coca-Cola, there was just enough for everyone to drink a small glassful. The taste of that fiery liquid was a solemn moment for Dick and me – a nostalgic memory of old times in Jugoslavia and a sort of pledge that we must protect and care for those fourteen homeless Croatians as best we could, never allow them to become victims of the English bloodsuckers lurking in the shadows and try to bring some sunshine into their lives.

Ada and I squeezed them all into the dining-room a few minutes later – she was not at all pleased to find the hangers-on sharing the meal as well – and she and I served the beef stew and potatoes and cauliflower she had cooked, followed by an apple crumble. Sadly they were too exhausted and, in some cases, feeling too ill to do justice to the meal; but when it was finished, Anica and Marica insisted on helping us with the washing-up no matter how hard we tried to prevent them.

Each family had decided upon which bedrooms they would occupy by eight o' clock, and Dick persuaded all the visitors to leave soon afterwards as we realized how much our people were longing to have some peace and a good night's sleep.

"They all seem very nice, don't they?" I remarked to Dick on the way home. "I didn't notice a single one who looked as if they might give trouble in the days ahead."

He agreed with me but suggested that we should not be too hard on the Mansfield crowd. "Most of them did, after all, go out to Croatia to fetch the refugees, so I suppose you can understand them not wanting to let go and hand them over to us too soon."

"Well, there's another twenty-three of them parked all over Mansfield. Let's hope they concentrate on those ones in the future," I murmured, the toy-trunk still nagging at me like an open sore.

Chapter 5 - Settling In

It was pouring with rain next day, and the flat was full of visitors. Anica greeted us with a big smile when we arrived after breakfast, but she seemed rather harassed and appeared even more exhausted than she had been the previous day.

Cynthia, who had called round there about eight o'clock, told us that Ivan (Katica's son) was running a temperature and some of the other children were complaining of violent toothache. Ada and her husband were already installed on the sofa in the big sitting-room, a shy young Irish priest occupied one of the armchairs and a reporter from the Nottingham Evening Post had pinioned Dragana against the window-sill to ask her a number of rather embarrassing questions. Down in the courtyard, meanwhile, a lorry had drawn up near the archway and some men were busy unloading innumerable sacks of coal while the NEP photographer leapt around urging them to stack the sacks in the shape of an isosceles triangle right outside the entrance to the flat.

"This is Father John Cairns who's recently come to look after our church in Ollerton," Ada introduced us. "And I'm sure we can arrange some transport to get all your families there on a Sunday; also I've spoken to the headmaster of the Roman Catholic school in Ollerton and he'll be delighted to receive the children at the beginning of next week."

Marica and Anica were behaving like true Croatian hostesses, brewing numerous cups of their precious Turkish coffee and offering them with biscuits to everyone in the sitting-room. Even though they had only just arrived in this strange new country, it would have been unthinkable for them not to offer refreshments to their guests.

"Have you spoken to the mothers about church?" I asked Ada, "I mean they might not all want to go."

The photographer burst into the room at that moment to announce that he was ready, and the reporter demanded that we should round up all the refugees and bring them out into the courtyard to have their photographs taken beside the coal heap.

Dick began to bristle like a badger with some uninvited animal in its lair. "You DO realize, I suppose, that all these poor people are completely exhausted after travelling non-stop right across Europe, and some of the children are not feeling at all well· this morning? Also it's pouring with rain outside and none of them have umbrellas."

Ada tried to soothe Dick by telling him that the photographs were only required for the Coal Board's benefit, to give them some good publicity as they were offering all this coal free; but that only seemed to make matters worse. We compromised in the end, with a few sacks of coal surrounded by the refugees under the cover of the archway; and I noticed that little blonde Ivana had been placed right in the forefront of the picture.

Dick and I left soon afterwards to take our dog for a walk in the forest. When we returned after lunch we found Mick and his friends with their wives and the two awful children sprawled about the sitting-room, while Janja and Anica, who looked at the end of their tether, served them with tea and cakes.

"We're going to have a moonthly get together for all the crowd we brought over from Croatia," one of the drivers informed us; "and as you've got a nice big place here with plenty of groob in the larder, we thought we'd hold our first one here next Soonday. There'll be aboot fifty of uz, boot we should fit in O.K. if we shifts a few bits of furniture out of this room."

"Have you asked the mothers yet, if they really want to have this party in their home?" I inquired, feeling waves of anger sweeping over me again. "After all, the food was put in their larder by some kind people round here for them to eat themselves."

"No point in asking 'em 'cos they doarn't speak our lingo," he snarled.

There was a crash further along the corridor just then, followed by some children shrieking and an angry girl's voice telling them to behave. It turned out to be the visiting brats, who had slunk out of the sitting-room when we arrived and pulled over a chest-of-drawers in one of the bedrooms; and the voice admonishing them was that of Marina, a Croatian girl who was billeted with one of the coach-drivers and his family in Mansfield, but was mortified by the way his children were allowed to carry on.

I met Anica and two of the mothers in the kitchen, and asked them if they wanted to have such a big party in their home in a few days' time. The answer was clearly "NO", but they did not wish to seem rude nor inhospitable to anyone who had brought them all the way from Croatia to England.

"No party here next Sunday," Dick told the Mansfield gang with great firmness. "Our mothers don't want it so you'd better have it in the church hall where Rosemary told us it had been arranged in the first place."

The battle of the wills was starting already, but Mick's next remark reduced us to silence.

"I forgot to tell you that we've got all the kids into the two best Roman Catholic schools in Mansfield – All Saints and St Philip Neri," he announced cheerfully. "And the headmaster has even managed to find a Croatian-speaking teacher to start 'em off with. I'm to roon their school booss service, and one of us'll be picking 'em up from here each morning."

"Trump card!" I whispered to Dick. "Wait till our Ada gets to hear about this!"

While all these pronouncements and arguments were taking place, Malcolm and Cynthia were working away quietly in the background, making appointments for the children at the doctor's clinic in Edwinstowe, showing the mothers how to work the vacuum and washing-machine and carrying up fresh supplies of coal and logs for the fires. Cynthia and Janja managed to understand each other although neither of them had a word of any language in common, and they became good friends right from the start.

*   *   *   *   *   *

The sun was shining next day. Dick and I drove across to the old stables after breakfast and took three of the mothers, Marica, Janja and Katica, to the little supermarket in the village of Ollerton.

Marica's family came, originally, from Hercegovina, but she had lived in the small town of Ilok, near Vukovar, for most of her life, and worked for twenty years or more in a textile factory there, along with her cousin, Anica. Marica's husband, Zvonimir, was a tractor driver before the Serbs arrived in October 1991, when the family were forced to leave their home and escape in a lorry to Slovenski Brod. They were put in a teeming refugee camp for ten days, before being sent to another one in Zagreb and, later, to Opatija on the Istrian coast where thousands of refugees were being housed in the big tourist hotels – with one room only per family.

Zvonimir was involved in a car crash and very badly injured. He had already undergone thirteen operations on one of his feet when the family were offered the chance of coming to England for six months. He had encouraged them to go, but remained in Croatia himself as he was waiting for yet another operation.

Marica was rather a shy person with a very sweet nature, and an overwhelming desire to cause no trouble to her English hosts. She and her two companions wandered around the supermarket in a bemused condition, asking for such unlikely goods as *'Vegetat'* and *'Jubilarna Kava,'* which caused a blank expression to appear on the faces of those they questioned. Janja soon took the lead, and after much thought, and pinching and prodding of items of interest, she advanced towards the till with her wire basket filled with potatoes, fruit and rice, and a fearless look in her eyes. A small crowd of local people had gathered near the cash desk to gaze at our refugees, and one of them ventured a few comments as we drew closer.

"Yon women looks spittin' image of thorse I saw in Chad today, Petal," he addressed the Cashier. "Shouldn't be surprised if they didn't coom wiv Mick Gelsthorpe all the way from Yoogorslavia."

He and his friends nodded intelligently and murmured a few words of welcome to our group and wished them well. Although the mothers could not understand a word they were saying, they felt a wave of warmth flowing towards them and Katica, beaming at the crowd with her sunniest smile, confided to me that England was full of nice people and she felt sure she would be happy here!

When we returned to the flat poor Marijana, who had violent toothache, was busy sweeping the long corridor while Anica was making coffee for a charming young reporter from the Retford Times. His photographer, meanwhile, was making sheep's eyes at Katica's daughter, Natali.

"Hope we're not causing too much trouble," he greeted us; "but I'd like to get a story and a few photographs for our next edition about your big family's first impressions of England – how they felt about coming to a strange country, what they think of the people and countryside here ... you know the sort of thing?"

I translated what he had said and, because he looked so sympathetic and rather shy, the mothers and children clustered round him to answer his questions and pose for some photographs.

"He's quite different to those men yesterday, with the bags of coal," Dragana whispered to me. "I hope he come again!"

The photographer suddenly announced that he intended to return in two days' time with some of his photographs to give to our children. Natali who, like her friend, Dragana, understood some English, promptly turned a rich shade of pink as the two young men said goodbye and clattered down the stairs.

All the other children were watching television in the sitting-room when Peter Leplar and John Hand, the President of the Nottinghamshire Rotary Club, came to call. My first thought was that our poor families would never get any peace nor a chance to cook their lunch. But I was soon to revise my opinion when Peter told us that he had made arrangements with three local factories to provide all the refugees with free wellington boots, woollen jumpers and several dresses each – all new stock from which they were invited to come and choose what they wanted as soon as possible.

We were told later that Mrs Sue Fowler of Jonathan James, Carter Lane in Mansfield had offered the fourteen pairs of wellingtons, and Mr Quentin Kopp, the Director of Mansfield Knitwear at Alfreton in Derbyshire, had provided all the woollen jumpers. But Dick and I were there ourselves on the day that Peter arranged the expedition to select the dresses and skirts from Etam, a clothing factory on the Boughton Industrial Estate near Newark.

The Croatians are a proud race, and although our families had arrived in England with little beyond the clothes they were wearing, some of them were already showing signs of embarrassment at receiving so many gifts.

Mr Anthony Hopkin was waiting for us at the factory entrance, and we were ushered into a large room filled with clothes-horses on which hung a big variety of tempting garments. We were then introduced to the manageress who explained that each person might select five different outfits if they wished, and would I please make this clear to our refugees.

I had hardly finished translating her message in my halting Croatian, before there was a wild charge by some of the teenage girls towards a horse filled with thigh-length, semi-transparent evening dresses. Natali, who has strong arms and swift feet, was the first to reach a little black number with a frilly lace pussy-pelmet, much to the fury of the other girls!

Anica, meanwhile, was fingering a long black skirt rather reluctantly and murmuring that one garment was all that she required – in fact, it would be more than enough as she already had her green dress from Zagreb for best.

There came a point where Dick and I had to intervene as some members of our party were already staggering under the weight of seven or eight hangers full of clothing, two boys appeared to be having a tug-of-war with a stylish pair of jeans and two other families were being left way behind in the clothing stakes.

"Think of going to church, of cold days in the winter, of party night at the village club," I urged them, while Dick grabbed a few garments off the mounds of dresses that were moving rapidly towards the exit on the far side of the room and, whispering *"Dosta, dosta!* (enough, enough!)" to those who were clutching them, he began to replace them on their clothes-horses.

We passed the manageress's scrutiny with some semblance of order and dignity in the end, and thankfully escaped to the waiting cars.

"Phew!" Dick murmured, as we drove away; "That certainly gave one an interesting insight into human nature!"

*   *   *   *   *   *

Katica was unlike any of the other mothers, in that she would take with open arms and a happy smile everything that was offered her. This conduct worked equally well in reverse, as she was always delighted to share her gifts with other people. Janja was made of sterner stuff and could look rather remote and fierce if she disapproved of someone's behaviour, while Marica and Anica often showed their reluctance to receive any new presents and would protest that we had given them far too much already.

Katica came, originally, from the small town of Otačac in Krajina. Her mother still lived there, very precariously, with the Serb shells raining down on the houses all around her. Big tears would often stream down her daughter's face when she watched the horrifying pictures on television news and thought of her mother in the midst of so much danger.

Katica's husband, Milan, was a Croat from Bački Brestovac in Serbia, and the family had moved to his home town in 1988. But only four years later the Jerbić's house and workshop and farm buildings were burnt to the ground by the advancing army. Katica, with their daughter, Natali, and son, Ivan, fled to Rijeka, while Milan walked for five days across the mountains to reach safety. Later on the family found themselves sharing the garage of a deserted villa on the Adriatic coast with Janja and her family who came from Slunj. But Milan was soon compelled to join the Croatian army, and he became a sergeant in charge of communications on the front line; so poor Katica had many worries, and her face was often streaked with tears during those early days at Thoresby.

*   *   *   *   *   *

We took five members of our new family shopping in the village of Edwinstowe a few days after their arrival. The intention was to buy fourteen pairs of bedroom slippers, but the small and tranquil shop in the High Street had seldom been confronted with such lively customers, all anxious to try on every pair of slippers on the shelves.

That same afternoon we gave a tea-party for nineteen in our house on the edge of the hamlet of Perlethorpe. *Butterfields* was built in 1986 and it is not a particularly big or grand house, having no more than three bedrooms, two bathrooms and four other rooms; but the drawing-room is exceedingly large as it was planned to receive some of Grandpa

Butterfield's furniture when Thoresby House was returned to the National Coal Board who had been our landlords for the past few years. There is a magnificent malachite and gilt mantelpiece, for instance, which had travelled from the Ural Mountains in Russia, via Florence, Yorkshire and Thoresby, to our new house. And there are two enormous marble-topped French commodes from the period of Napoleon III (it took eight men to lift each one), a tall marquetry glass-fronted cabinet and a matching bureau, two large gilt-framed sofas and a number of chairs of similar style, as well as Grandpa's grand piano and several huge pictures.

Dick fetched our four families in a large Land Rover belonging to the Home Farm, while Amelia, Eileen, Vera and I prepared tea. All three are old friends of ours whom we hoped might feel sympathetic towards the refugees. Amelia Lorenzo Navaza comes from La Coruña in Northern Spain, and although she has lived at Thoresby for nearly thirty years, she was only too well aware of the hostile reception given to foreigners by many English people who have never left their own country. She lives in a cottage very close to the old stables, so was one of the Croatian's nearest neighbours, along with Bill and Anne Judkins who lived next door.

I forget in which order the refugees entered the house, but I clearly

Amelia Lorenzo Navaza

Bill Judkins

remember Anica leading the way into the drawing-room, closely followed by the other mothers and their daughters, while the boys lingered in the hall to examine Dick's collection of old pistols, guns and swords.

"Holy Mother of Jesus!" she exclaimed. "This is a real *Gospodar's* home – a type of castle, you understand? Some of you may have witnessed such places on *Amerikanski* television? Take note of the furniture, the mantelpiece, the pictures," she commanded her audience, throwing her arms wide open to embrace the whole room.

Anica wore an emerald-green silk dress and elegant black shoes which suited her ideally. Her brown eyes shone and her long dark hair flew out in a flurry of excitement while she drank in her surroundings. The other three mothers advanced cautiously into the room with their daughters following close behind them, their wide-open, rather anxious eyes darting swiftly from right to left. I overheard Marica instructing her two youngest children in a harsh whisper to follow her closely, touch nothing and behave like saints ... if not, she would inform Papa in her next letter.

We introduced Amelia, Eileen and Vera to our guests, then Amelia and I went to fetch the tea-tray while Dick persuaded the Croatians to sit down. Dosco, our huge black Newfoundland dog, had forged his way through the back door while our backs were turned, and he exploded into the drawing-room about that time and galloped round the room sniffing everyone joyfully. Janja, and her daughter, Dragana, stood their ground heroically, but Katica, Natali and Anica emitted shrieks of terror which excited Dosco even further. He was just about to put both front paws on Katica's shoulders when Dick grabbed him by the collar and hauled him outside into the garden.

Ivan, Katica's little boy, had recovered from his fever by then, and he and Dragan came into the room and sat down gingerly on a pair of brocade-covered tiny gilt chairs, as the sofas and larger chairs were already occupied by the womenfolk. Dragan looked around him and rolled his eyes so that the dark brown corneas almost disappeared from sight, and the whites gleamed brilliantly in the lamplight.

Amelia, Eileen and I brought in the hot buttered crumpets and scones, a big selection of cakes and three teapots. A sepulchral silence descended on the room as we poured out and passed round the cups, milk and sugar. Dick helped offer the crumpets and scones, and attempted a few tentative jokes, but there was a marked shortage of conversational flow and even Dragana and Natali, the only two who spoke some English, had retreated into a silent reverie; and the smaller children, with their mother's eyes boring into them, were so beautifully behaved that they hardly dared open their mouths to receive any food!

My throat completely dried up, and the few polite Croatian phrases that I had rehearsed beforehand seemed to have deserted me. I gazed anxiously round the room and received some lightning impressions: Marijana, Marica's eighteen-year-old daughter, looked rather sad and held the right side of her face as she was still in great pain from her tooth-ache – she had an appointment to see the dentist next day; her little sister, Ivana, had a sweet nature, I felt convinced, which would not be spoilt by her good looks; Marjan, Anica's son, appeared remote and might be difficult? Dragan ...

My thoughts were interrupted by Dick with his camera, which proved to be the turning-point in that silent tea-party. Although our guests had eaten less than sparrows, they all loved having their photographs taken and posed most willingly in family groups in front of the log fire.

"Please can I have a copy to send to my mother in Krajina?" Katica asked him, and when he promised to get extra copies for all the mothers their faces lit up with pure delight.

Amelia and Eileen, meanwhile, had succeeded in sowing the first seeds of what was to become a deep and lasting friendship with Anica and Marica – although how they managed without a word of any language in common, I shall never know.

"Would you like to see the rest of the house?" Dick suggested, after the photographic session was over.

Ivan with Katica.

He led the way from one room to another, and I pointed out the best paintings of Jugoslavia that my mother had done some years ago. Then we all went upstairs so that our guests could see the view over the village of Perlethorpe and Thoresby Park. And while we were there, with most of our noses pressed to the window-panes, Dragan happened to notice Dick's collection of tiny model cars and a rather special motor bike which was

First visit to our kitchen. Back row: Marjan, Anica, Janja, Katica, Dragana, Antonija and Marica.
Front row: Josip, Marijana, Natali, Ivan, Damir and Ivana.

also a cigarette-lighter. Dick, who was in the bedroom fetching his handkerchief, came out just in time to see Dragan slip the motor bike into his pocket after glancing around hurriedly to make sure his mother was looking out of the window.

Anica wanted to go to the lavatory, so I showed her the door between the dining-room and kitchen, and she disappeared inside. Dick came downstairs about the same time and, waiting for the others to pass him, he intercepted Dragan who was the last one down. He tapped the boy's bulgy right pocket and said; "Can I have it back, please?"

Dragan's face had turned the colour of a beetroot as he hastily pulled out the lighter and handed it to Dick. After a brief pause my husband held it out for him to take again, and said; "A present for you."

That small incident was the beginning of a perfect understanding between Dragan and Dick, and the boy never betrayed his trust again despite all the exciting weaponry in our hall which was a source of great temptation to him and the other boys – even little Damir, aged six.

When the time came for our guests to go home, Bill Judkins, who had come to fetch Amelia, offered to take three in his car while Dick took the

Dosco

others. They were all collected near the front door in their overcoats saying *"Puno hvala* (Many thanks)" and *"Do vidjenja* (Goodbye)", when Vera commented; "There's one missing, I think. Wasn't there a lady in a green dress called Anica?"

I noticed that Dosco had crept back into the house and stretched himself across the floor between the dining-room and kitchen, with an evil glint in his eye. Then we saw the lavatory door open a few inches to allow a frightened face to appear in the crack for a moment, before the door was finally closed again. I grabbed the mischievous beast's collar and hauled him into the kitchen, then we all began to laugh and Antonija called to her mother that it was safe to come out at last!

Chapter 6 - 27 Kisses

Although our tea-party had been a testing ordeal for everyone concerned, it had broken the ice in a number of unforeseen ways and introduced the Croatians to a few other people in the neighbourhood who were to play a big part in their lives in the months ahead. But there was one rather worrying aspect of their early days in the Stables' flat over which we had little control.

"The cars of the Mansfield gang were in the courtyard again last night," Cynthia reported next morning. "And they stayed till well after midnight, as they were still there when Malcolm and I went to bed."

"Well, there's nothing much we can do about it," we told her; "except ask the mothers if they really want to have those visitors till late every night. If they say "No", we'll turn our Stan on to them!"

Stan Hodgkinson is the Head Keeper, and few people feel inclined to linger on Thoresby territory if he tells them to leave.

Janja and Anica spread out their hands with the palms upturned when we asked them, and Janja said "We do not wish to offend Mick and his friends if they want to come here. It was, after all, they who drove all the way to Croatia to bring us back here, and *Veliki John* (Big John) is always welcome as he does many good things for our children."

Whenever we coincided with the Mansfield gang we noticed that he was usually at the centre of a circle of children, organizing games for them and producing much laughter and happiness. Some of the others, however, would stride into the flat as if they owned it, help themselves to apples or oranges from the fruit bowl without asking permission or waiting for an invitation, then light up their cigarettes and fill the sitting-room with smoke – none of the Croatians were smokers – while they settled down in the best armchairs to watch television. And if by any chance it was lunch or supper-time, they took it for granted that they would be sharing the meal with our mothers and children.

The Mansfield gang were not, however, the only visitors in the early days. There were several other regular ones who came out of the goodness of their hearts or because they grew very fond of the people they were visiting; and they usually brought gifts or invitations to the refugees to drive them to the shops or to see the countryside, and sometimes to their own homes for a meal. There was a wonderful lady called Joan Seager who ran the Dukeries Host Association, set up to look after foreign students who came to study in England and had no friends nor contacts with whom to share their leisure. Although she could not communicate with our families, except through Dragana and Natali, she would often come to Thoresby and sit peacefully in the sitting-room with them, if no one wished to go out for a drive in her car. Our neighbour, Betty Briggs, was another angel of mercy who brought twelve fresh loaves of bread, week after week, to the Stables' flat.

There was also John Gradiški, who had been one of the interpreters in Mick's coach when they set off on their November mission to Croatia and brought back the thirty-seven refugees. He came over to Thoresby on the third day to see how our families were getting along, and wrote the Croatian names under the English ones on all the tinned food in their larder. There were many problems that he was able to help us sort out in the months ahead, and he and his English wife, as well as his friends in the Croatian Society, based in Derby, did a great deal to stem the waves of homesickness felt by our mothers during their first Christmas in a strange land.

Rowan McFerran's wife, Janet, is in charge of the Pierrepont Gallery in the old Stables at Thoresby, and thanks to her drive, enthusiasm and sheer hard work, she has made a fantastic success of the whole enterprise which had only started in September, 1991. Realizing what a boon it would be for our mothers if they could understand some English and talk to their neighbours, she promptly found an English teacher for them at Worksop College, the school where her own sons were educated.

Kathy Beckett agreed to come over to Thoresby twice a week, after school hours, to give a lesson free of charge to our little group. Sometimes the lesson would take place in Janet's house and at other times in the house of a neighbour, Gilda Prest, to give the Croatians a chance to escape from their overcrowded flat; also to drink coffee and make conversation in some English homes. I think Anica and Katica profited most from those lessons, but occasionally there was a kind of blockage when no one wanted to learn any English. Perhaps they were missing home too much and the families they had left behind them, and were counting the days till they could return; or they may have felt that they were being bossed around more than they could tolerate after their children had gone to school?

Cynthia was undoubtedly the prime 'bosser', and although she could not utter a word of Croatian she had no difficulty in making herself clearly understood. On the third morning she pinned up a large piece of white paper on the inner door of the flat. It was divided into seven columns, one for each day of the week, and in each column she would write with bold red letters any engagements or appointments for that particular day. She would then tower over the mother concerned and roar at her, "You go to dentist at ten o'clock, understand?"

It was a brave women or child who put up any resistance to that treatment, which was often accompanied by a display of tooth-tapping, imitation extractions and holding of the face in pain; but it was never very effective with Janja. She stood six feet tall herself and could glare at Cynthia, eyeball to eyeball, so to speak, over any contentious issues!

But these were few and far between, because she really liked Cynthia and was very grateful for all the trouble she and Malcolm took to look after them.

Without those particular guardians, we often wondered how our fourteen mothers and children would have managed after our return to London, as we were only able to spend a third of our time at *Butterfields*. The dentist's appointments and the children's schooling had been taken care of by Mick and his friends, and any mother needing to visit the dentist had to go on the school bus leaving for Mansfield early that morning, and hang around there all day until the bus returned in the late afternoon. Although Mick had scored some valuable points on those issues, Ada remained firmly in charge of religion and made sure that a mini-bus (paid for by the parishioners of her church in Ollerton) called regularly at the Stables every Sunday morning to bring her flock to church!

But there were plenty of other engagements: visits to the doctor's surgery in Edwinstowe, shopping expeditions to the cheapest supermarkets, evenings out at the village hall when there was a dance taking place, or to bingo in Worksop, all of which were organized by Malcolm and Cynthia; and they made a point of calling at the flat at least twice each day to find out if there were any fresh *problemas* looming since their last visit.

*   *   *   *   *   *

November 13th was a special day for Dick and me, as we had been invited to lunch by our four families. We arrived at the flat to find the dining-room laid with all the best china and glassware, and some of our favourite dishes cooking on the stove in the kitchen.

"*Divno!*" Dick declared, inhaling happily. "It feels just like being back on holiday in Croatia."

"We cannot prepare for you the dishes we would desire you to eat," Marica explained, her shoulders rising dramatically to indicate their lack of resources and the special herbs they had been unable to purchase in the local supermarket. "But we wish to say a big 'thank-you' from our hearts for the welcome we have received here, and to tell you that we now regard you as our father and mother."

This sentence was delivered to me in Croatian, which I then attempted to translate for Dick's benefit while Dragana's eyes bored into me – clearly she did not trust my ability to render the true meaning of those words. There followed a few moments of silence while we digested the importance of what Marica had just said.

It was that same day when all the kissing first began! My old English/Croatian phrase book advised quite severely; "Don't forget to shake hands when greeting or leaving people. Jugoslavs often shake hands in social contacts, and frequently kiss as well."

Well, I cannot recall who delivered the first kiss, but we soon realized that each person expected to receive two kisses, one on each cheek, grown-ups and children alike; and you did not just do this once a day when you first converged, but each time you met and each time you

Dosco with Marijana, Damir and Ivana near the old stables. Winter 1992

parted, even if there was only a five minute interval in between. For the normally cold and reserved Anglo-Saxon this was quite an eye-opener; but also one that was filled with sharp impressions as you closed in on your next victim!

Dragan, for instance, always rolled his eyes, exhibiting mainly the whites, when it was his turn; Ivana looked really pleased to greet you and little Damir refused to give two kisses, but opted for a full frontal on the mouth instead. Counting up some days later, I calculated that we were totting up twenty-seven kisses each, whenever we visited the old stables; and twenty-seven more when we left to go home!

*   *   *   *   *   *

After our Croatian lunch-party, Dick and I borrowed the farm Land Rover once again, and we drove twelve of our party to visit the Queen Oak in the heart of Sherwood Forest. The legend of Robin Hood appeared to be as famous in the Balkans as it was in Nottinghamshire, and we sensed a keen air of excitement as we approached the old oak tree inside which he had lived.

It was a cold grey autumn day with not a tourist in sight. The gnarled branches of the ancient trees formed a canopy between the dead grey sky and the dead red leaves which lay thick as a pile carpet on the ground. Ivan and Dragan hid in the hollow of a neighbouring tree to cause their mothers to bellow with fear when their absence was noticed. But the girls stayed close to us asking, with big round eyes, if there were still bandits or wolves or bears living in the woods.

We took photographs of our big family in front of the Queen Oak and Anica said; "I shall be able to settle with more peace of mind when I receive my first letter from home and know that my family are receiving my letters also. Then we can send pictures of our life in England for all to see!"

Anica was a great letter-writer, and we posted three or four each day for her when she was unable to get to a post office herself. She was born in Vukovar, but had lived all her life in the neighbouring small town of Ilok where she used to work in a textile factory, along with her cousin, Marica.

The Serbs arrived in October 1991, and forced the Hržić family to leave their home. Anton, her husband, was put in a detention camp, but Antonija, his thirteen-year-old daughter, pleaded with the guards to release him and, after one week, the whole family fled in a lorry to Zagreb. They stayed with Anton's sister for nearly ten months, but there were five extra people in a house which was only intended for one family; so they decided to move to a refugee hotel at Opatija on the Istrian coast in August 1992. And there they remained, the five of them living in one room, until Mick arrived with his coach and offered them the chance to come to England.

Anton encouraged his family to go, but men of his age were not allowed to leave Croatia; and shortly after their departure he was called up and sent to the front line as an ambulance driver. Poor Anica! There were many tears shed when she heard the news, and a feeling of being torn in two halves: on the one hand it was important to provide the best life possible for her three children but, on the other hand, she felt she had deserted her husband, her old mother and her brother and two sisters back at home.

The first two or three weeks were filled with health care, settling into new schools, religion (ably taken care of by our Ada) and Social Security forms. There was a half-Polish, half-Croatian girl called Meggi who worked for the local Social Services Department and was an excellent interpreter, so the refugees were put under her wing. When there were any problems she was helped by Ada who always knew the right people to approach. The result was far better than we had dared to hope for, as each mother received about £5 per person per day, allowing her to buy enough food for her family with a little extra for clothing or other expenses. The flat was rent free, and we had agreed to be responsible for the electricity, milk, bread, television licence and telephone bills during the first six months.

The most violent toothaches and fevers had subsided, and our huge bewildered new family were gradually settling into their English home when we left them to return to London on November 15th.

Chapter 7 - Winter Days

Our vicar at St John's Church, Perlethorpe, the Reverend John Williams, produced a jewel of an idea the day after the Croatian's arrival in Thoresby Park.

"Do you think your families would like to become a bit more mobile and have some bicycles to ride?" he asked. "It is, after all, three miles to the nearest village with any shops in it, and they might not always want to depend on other people to drive them to and fro."

"I'm sure they'd love it," I replied; "and even if they don't know how to ride them, I expect the young ones would soon learn."

We forgot about that conversation till our return to Thoresby some two weeks later. It was a frosty morning towards the end of November when Dick and I arrived in the Stables' courtyard to find the vicar greeting a man who had just pulled up in a large van.

"Let me introduce Mr Martin Shaw from Center Parcs," he said. "And I think you'd better get everyone downstairs before he opens the van doors!"

Little Damir had already appeared, and he called up the stairs to all the other children to come down quickly as there was something unusual about to spring out of this strange *vagon,* but he couldn't be sure what it was. There were ten children clustered round the vicar a few minutes later, two mothers hanging out of upstairs windows and Marica hissing at Damir to behave himself, otherwise he would not be allowed to take part in this mysterious business in the courtyard.

Mr Shaw strolled round to the back of the van, opened the doors and lifted out the first bicycle: there was a pause of about two seconds and a sharp intake of breath from ten open mouths, followed by a noise like gas escaping from a punctured pipe. Dragan had placed himself in a commanding position to be the first to see inside the van, so he received the first bicycle and Ivana was right behind him in line for the next one. It proved, however, to be a male machine and Mr Shaw said there were nine others specially intended for females. Before she had time to batter Josip over the head he had seized it from her and was already riding away at full speed round the courtyard in pursuit of Dragan.

The wonderful Mr Shaw had brought fourteen bicycles as a gift from Center Parcs where our vicar acted as Chaplain, and it soon transpired that everyone knew how to ride one except Janja and little Damir, whose legs were too short to reach the pedals which made him roar with anger. I attempted to give some severe advice in Croatian about not going outside the courtyard as the roads were dangerous and very slippery; but no one paid the slightest attention and a moment later nine of the bicycles had disappeared, Marica was trying to comfort her furious son and Katica and Anica were shouting "*Supair! Prima!*" as they raced round the courtyard at top speed on two of the larger machines.

"No need to wonder if they will be a success," the vicar laughed. "I think we can safely leave them to sort out the sizes and who has which bicycle."

"But how about the poor little bloke crying his eyes out under the archway?" demanded Mr Shaw. "We'll have to see what we can do about him."

True to his word, he drove into the Stables' courtyard again two days later, bringing with him a fairy-cycle which was just the right size for Damir. Ivan and Josip soon taught him how to ride it, and he was supremely proud of himself when fifteen of us set off on our bicycles to explore the forest a few weeks later.

Janja, who had no inclination to learn, stayed behind to cook the lunch. She seldom showed signs of the deep emotions which plunged the other women into the depths of despair from time to time, although I am sure she suffered as much as any of them in her own quiet way. She was a hard worker with a strong character, and she was well able to stand up to anyone who caused her distress.

Janja and her husband, Filip, had kept a *gostionica* (a small guest-house) at Slunj in the Plitvice National Park where there are some famous waterfalls which were very popular among the tourists before the war. The Serb soldiers arrived in July 1991 and set fire to their home, so they were forced to flee to Slovenia where they lived with Janja's sister-in-law for six months. At the end of that period the Slovenian authorities ordered them to leave because their country was being overrun by the ever-increasing hordes of Croatian refugees. They were sent to a refugee hostel in one of the coastal towns near Rijeka and, shortly afterwards, found themselves sharing an underground garage with Katica and Milan and their two children. It was during those dark days amid the diesel fumes that the two girls, Dragana and Natali, became best friends and, later on, were to beg Mick not to separate their two families when they came to England.

*   *   *   *   *   *

The second get-together of the thirty-seven refugees was planned to take place in a church-hall in Mansfield Woodhouse on November 28th. Mick had told our families to be ready at seven o'clock, when he would send transport to fetch them. They knew that most of the other mothers and children would be there with their English hosts, and they begged us to come too – and take as many of them as possible in our car.

"What's wrong with Mick's transport?" I asked Natali. "He fetches you and brings you back from school every day, after all."

"Me no like Mick's bus. Driver, he never stop smoking and he take funny route to Mansfield. Not straight one, you understand?"

This statement was accompanied by a big play of hands sweeping aside invisible clouds of smoke, then gripping the seat as the bus negotiated rough terrain.

"We'll have to look into that," Dick promised the girl. "We're due to meet your headmaster next week anyway, and we'll see what he can do about the school bus."

We arrived at the church-hall to find the party in full swing. The vicar of St Edmund's Church and his devoted band of helpers had prepared a tasty buffet supper, and there was a warm and friendly atmosphere, music, dancing and games for the children like Hunt the Slipper and Musical Chairs, which the grown-ups appeared to enjoy as much as the little ones. John Gradiški and other members of the Croatian Society were there, along with Meggi and most of the coach drivers and their friends who went out to Croatia to fetch the refugees.

We were introduced to various mothers and their children while we sat, surrounded by our own big family, on the edge of the dance-floor. There was a very nice schoolteacher from Dubrovnik who already spoke good English; and another young woman with two small children who was lodged with a local doctor and his wife. And there was Biljana, who had the most striking face of anyone in that crowded hall. A girl in her early twenties, she resembled an ivory-skinned Madonna with long brown hair and huge dark eyes which stared into space, devoid of all hope. Two pale and sickly children clung to her skirt – a boy of three and a younger girl – each one demanding her entire attention as they had no desire to play with the other children in the hall.

Anica told me her story on the way home. The Serbs had come to

Biljana's village a year ago and dragged her young husband from his bed in the middle of the night. She and the children ran out after him to find him being tortured, then murdered in front of their eyes. All the men in that village were slaughtered in the most brutal ways, and when the women and children fled their burnt-out homes after the soldiers had gone, they were faced with one last horror: the village butcher, a neighbour and good friend of all who lived there, had been crucified and left suspended, upside-down, by the side of the road leading to safety.

No wonder poor Biljana stared ahead into an abyss of nothingness; and she had been unlucky with her placing in England, as she found herself and her children occupying a freezing cold attic room with no one to talk to in her own language, and no means of keeping warm or cooking her own food while the lady of the house was out at work; and she was not inclined to be sympathetic when she was at home. There were several other families who had struck equally bad homes, and they felt so lonely and unhappy that they asked to go back to the refugee hostels in their own country after a few weeks had passed. I think many English people started off with kind and generous intentions – or perhaps they enjoyed the initial publicity and felt superior to their neighbours who had watched the same horror pictures on television news, but did nothing for the poor refugees beyond sorting out a few old clothes.

Two of the main problems were the food and language barriers. Our cooking seemed bland and tasteless to the Balkan palate, although the children soon developed a liking for chips. When the families had the use of a stove and could do their own cooking, like at the Stables' flat, there was no problem; but the language barrier was a deeper issue and could lead to all kinds of misunderstandings between the host families and their refugees. I often wondered why the English people had not purchased English/Croatian dictionaries right at the beginning; but the idea of making the effort to communicate in some foreign language was anathema to many people we knew!

*   *   *   *   *   *

"How many of you have your own passports?" Dick asked the four mothers during our next visit to the Stables' flat.

Janja proved to be the only one, and hers had been kept by the Immigration Authorities at Dover when she first landed in England. Anica, Marica and Katica and their children had had their names inscribed on a sheet of paper, along with the other refugees who travelled with Mick from Croatia. That was their only means of identification, and he told us

that they must all travel back to Croatia together on a certain date next
May, six months after their arrival in this country.

"Supposing the war has not finished and you have no homes to which
you can return? You might not wish to go back to the refugee hostels?" I
suggested.

They saw the point immediately, and were very grateful to Dick that he
should have offered to try and get them all their own passports. This
entailed much hard work and expense. There were many telephone calls to
the Croatian Embassy in London and the Immigration Authorities in
Croydon, and endless forms to fill in which contained some rather tricky
questions. John Gradiški came over to help us interpret them, as we had
been warned that giving the wrong answers to questions like "Why do you
wish to live in England?" could cause plenty of trouble for our families if
one was not very careful. It was many weeks later that the passports
(costing about £70 each) finally arrived, but long before then Dick had
suggested to Mick Gelsthorpe that he should try to do the same for the
other mothers he had brought to Mansfield.

He and his friends still came to the flat almost every evening, expecting
a meal and the use of the sitting-room until late at night. Janja and her
family would leave the room and retire into her bedroom with a slam of
the door as soon as they arrived, and I think Katica often followed suit.

Our own relationship with the Mansfield gang, apart from 'Big John',
was also deteriorating, but the final explosion did not occur until after
Christmas.

*   *   *   *   *   *

Damir and his sister, Ivana, had made some special friends just round the
corner from home. Amelia and her little dog, Judy, and Bill Judkins who
lived next door, were always out in their garden to wave the children
goodbye when the school bus drove past each morning, taking them to
Mansfield. And when it returned in the late afternoon, Damir and Ivana
would often run round to Amelia's cottage to stroke Judy and drink Coca
Cola with their new friends.

Damir's English was progressing very fast and one day he said to
Amelia; "Me like your house. Can we see upstairs, please?"

Amelia led the way to the top of the house and took him into every room
to show him some of her treasures. When they reached her bedroom, he
paused in front of the dressing-table and gazed at the photograph of a
young girl, taken some forty years ago in Spain. After a few thoughtful
minutes he turned round and looked intently at Amelia.

"You very pretty girl! I can see that now," he announced, his large dark eyes filled with admiration.

He often told Amelia about his adventures at school. He had enjoyed himself there, right from the first day; and when we asked him why, he replied, "Nice dinner!" – and rubbed his tummy appreciatively.

A few weeks later he revealed to Amelia that a gang of boys had surrounded him in the playground that morning and started hitting him.

"And what did you do, my poor little treasure?" Amelia asked, fetching him a Mars Bar to eat.

"Me tell them to fuck off!" Damir replied, feeling rather proud of himself, but astonished at the effect this had on his Spanish friend.

"Good Lord! You must NOT use such words," she commanded him. "What would your mother say if she heard such language?"

"*Engleski* kids say same words, every day," he pouted, leaving her to ponder on his growing knowledge of the English language.

Dragana and Natali were also experiencing some tough moments at school during those first few weeks, and Natali sometimes came home in floods of tears. They complained that the girls in their class sneered and made fun of them, suggesting that they came from a backward, Third World country; and yet they themselves, they assured us, were at least a year ahead of their English class-mates in general knowledge, and Dragana worried incessantly that she would fall behindhand in her studies and be unable to catch up with girls of her own age when she returned to Croatia.

"Can you picture it! One of our teachers had his feet up on his desk yesterday, and he was smoking a cigarette," Dragana declared. "Such a thing would never happen in our schools."

A few days later we found ourselves seated in the Headmaster's office, along with Janja, Katica, Marica and Anica – also the Deputy Head and a rather attractive secretary.

"It's very kind of you to have arranged this meeting when we know how exceedingly busy you must be," Dick addressed the Headmaster in a soothing voice, hoping to create a tranquil atmosphere before broaching the reasons for our visit.

Mr Warley was tall and powerfully built, and he exuded an aura of unquestionable authority and a practised ease at dealing with complex situations which might have caused irritation to a lesser man. All Saints' R.C. Comprehensive School in Mansfield was, he claimed, the most popular Roman Catholic school in Nottinghamshire and, furthermore, parents would bring their children from miles around, even from across the Yorkshire and Derbyshire borders, if they heard there was a chance to enrol them in his school.

"We have over a thousand children already," he informed us. "And we are becoming desperately short of space and are seeking a government grant to build some more class-rooms. But that's a long story which I'm sure you have no wish to hear about at present, so pray tell me what I can do for you?"

His eyes were like searchlights scanning the coastal defences along a hostile shore. They rested briefly upon each person in turn, and I formed the impression that Janja met with his approval – perhaps he sensed a strength of character equal to his own in that tall dark foreigner, dressed in her best clothes, sitting upright in her chair and meeting his gaze unflinchingly.

Mr Warley dealt with the problem of the school bus in a few moments, agreeing with us that the driver should not be allowed to smoke, and if he was taking a less-than-direct route to school, for whatever reasons, he must be replaced at once. He instructed his Deputy to telephone the department which dealt with school transport in the local Education Authority, and ask them to offer the contract to another company, starting from next Monday.

"We do not tolerate any bullying in this school," he stressed, after hearing about the unhappiness of Natali and Dragana in their class. "The reason they suffer some insults from the girls around them is quite simple. It is because they are better-looking than most, so naturally the boys make sheep's eyes at them! Thus, it stands to reason that the local girls have become jealous and resentful of them. But I shall speak to their class teacher and instruct her to keep a close watch on the situation."

Dragana's worries about falling a year behind in her school studies were soon resolved when the Headmaster told us that they could not yet understand English well enough to study maths, science, history, etc, with their normal class, so they were spending much of their time with Monica, a Polish teacher he had engaged expressly for their benefit. She also spoke Croatian, and was concentrating on teaching her new pupils to learn and understand the English language above all else.

After this was explained to Janja by Monica herself, who had been summoned to the Headmaster's office at that stage, Dick and I decided to keep our mouths firmly shut on the subject of the smoking teacher with his feet up on the desk! We felt, and I think the four mothers did too, that their children were in good hands; and although there were bound to be some teething troubles, they were lucky to have been offered places in such an excellent secondary school where they had taken the trouble to find a Croatian-speaking teacher to help them during their first few months.

Marijana, who was eighteen, went to a special college of further education in Mansfield, and the younger children attended a Catholic primary school, St Philip Neri, not far from the secondary school. There were no complaints from that quarter, nor from Anica's daughter, Antonija, who was also a pupil at All Saints' School. Her youngest boy, Josip, got on very well in his class and, we heard much later, was in the habit of having the most engaging conversations with Mr Warley and his secretary, once his English had improved.

Marjan, Anica's eldest son, was the biggest *problema*. We had noticed when he first arrived that he was rather silent and withdrawn. His mother told us that he loved horses and had been able to ride in the old days, when they lived on a farm near Ilok. The Farm Manager at Thoresby had an old horse which his daughter-in-law rode at the weekends, and we introduced her to Marjan hoping that she might allow him to help with feeding and grooming the animal and cleaning out his stable. This proved to be a great success, and she very kindly arranged for him to ride the horse every Saturday morning while she ran along behind instructing him in how to grip the saddle and hold the reins.

She must have been a saint, that girl, for Saturday was her only free day as she worked hard in an office all week; and Marjan's English hardly improved at all during the first few months. I think he hated the whole concept of having deserted his own country and being forced to live abroad while such terrible things were happening at home.

Marjan looked very like his mother – the same fine features, smooth olive-brown skin and emotional eyes – and I sometimes had the most interesting conversations with him in Croatian. But he made very few friends of his own age, and had no capacity for childish games nor the intense *joie de vivre* which Josip, Damir and Ivan often displayed when they were not under the stern surveillance of their mothers. He did, however, have a complete understanding and love of our dog, Dosco.

"I've seldom seen such beautifully behaved children," Ada commented, on one of her regular visits to the refugees' flat. "I wish a few of our English parents could learn some lessons from these ones! It's quite extraordinary how the children are brought up to obey the word of command implicitly."

Chapter 8 - The New Year

The Christmas season passed in a whirl of visitors bearing food parcels and toys for the children, parties arranged by the Rotary Club and the Croatian Society and the arrival of reporters from many of the local newspapers seeking stories about how our families felt, spending their first Christmas far away from home and their loved ones. Marjan's birthday occurred on the same day as one of these visits, and a young photographer from the Mansfield Chad captured all the mothers and most of their children clustered around Marjan's cake, with Damir trying to blow out the thirteen candles in one breath.

Marjan's birthday party - 21st December 1992.
Left to right - Back row - Katica, Marica, Janja, Anica and Marijana.
Front row - Natali, Dragana, Antonija, Damir, Marjan and Ivan.
Photo: Courtesy of Mansfield Chad Newspapers

Ivana was photographed for the Nottingham Evening Post on Christmas Eve. She was holding the candle of peace and a reporter wrote the following article about her:

"Thousands of miles from home a young girl lights a candle of peace.

"Eleven-year-old Ivana Ðerd is safe and warm by the Christmas tree at Thoresby Hall in Nottinghamshire.

"A world away, her home village of Ilok, near Vukovar in Croatia, is torn apart by the civil war raging in the former Yugoslavia.

Rescued from Fighting

"Ivana, along with her mother Marica, sister Marijana, 18, and brother Damir, 6, have been rescued from the fighting by volunteers from Notts. Women and children from three other families share rooms above the stables at Thoresby.

"Ivana's father Zvonko, is still in Croatia and has been injured in the fighting. The little Croatian schoolgirl is hoping that he will get a phone call through to her on Christmas Day – she would love to wish him a happy Christmas.

"But Ivana will share a greater wish with the other Croatian families when they attend a local midnight mass tonight ... to be back with her father, in a peaceful world."

Another newspaper commented that it seemed very appropriate for the refugees to be living in an old stable, just as Jesus had done nearly two thousand years ago.

Three mothers came to our Carol Service in the little church at Perlethorpe, and Marica spent many hours crocheting a beautiful altar-cloth to give to the Vicar, to thank him for the bicycles which had transformed their lives.

The villagers of Perlethorpe had mixed feelings about the refugees, but they could at least count on a few special friends to help them in times of need. There were, first and foremost, Malcolm and Cynthia, who visited them twice each day, mended their household appliances whenever they went wrong, drove those who were feeling ill to the doctor's surgery in Edwinstowe in our absence, took several shopping and to Bingo in Worksop each week, or to the Village Hall when there was a party or dance going on.

Anica and Marica and their children had soon made friends with Amelia

Ted and Eileen Tivey

and Bill in the Stables' Cottages, and Ted and Eileen Tivey who lived in the village. They also received regular visits from Ada and Wilf, Joan Seager, John Gradiški, Meggi and Monica, their teacher at All Saints' School, as well as Millka, a Slovenian girl who taught in Damir's school, and her husband, Alojz. Various members of the local Rotary Club called in from time to time; also Patricia, a delightful girl who often brought them a present of fresh eggs from the egg factory where she worked.

John the Bee, on the other hand, who lived in the next-door flat at the Stables, never felt inclined to say "Good morning" when greeted by one of the women in the courtyard; and I suspect a number of people in the village harboured equally unfriendly feelings about their new neighbours.

"Fucking foreigners! We don't want our countryside crowded out with the likes of them, taking our Social Benefit money and cluttering up our housing list when there's hundreds of English families what needs a bit of money spending on them," was the opinion voiced by one old woman in the Newark area. She was well looked after by her husband and grown-up children, and had never lacked for anything, as far as we knew.

I sometimes wondered how it must feel to lose your home and all your clothes, furniture and the special household gods you have cherished all your life – as well as some of your dearest friends and relatives who have been murdered in cold blood in front of your eyes. Then to be taken far

away and put down in a strange land where you cannot understand what is
going on around you, and you are completely at God's mercy as to the
type of people who surround you. Will they make friends with you in due
course and forgive your shortcomings, or will they pass you by on the
other side of the street with a look of hatred in their eyes?

*   *   *   *   *   *

Two mattresses collapsed completely after six weeks' use, and Marica and
Katica, who shared their beds with their youngest children, were
beginning to complain of violent backaches when I took them to have a
check-up with the doctor in Edwinstowe. He wrote out a prescription for
some pain-killers and told me the probable cause of the trouble, so Dick
and I drove to Worksop and purchased two new mattresses the following
day. Considering that all the beds were second-hand, we felt relieved that
only two had caved in so far.

The arrival of the new mattresses caused quite a festive atmosphere in
the flat. Anica, Malcolm and Alan Bull, the Under Agent, all offered to
help carry them upstairs, and as soon as they had negotiated the steep
staircase and one or two sharp corners, the children crowded into the
rooms to sample the beds and Marica poured out little glasses of *Maraška*
(cherry brandy) with which to drink a toast to the mattresses. Seeing the
bedrooms again for the first time since we had furnished them last October
made us realize how overcrowded our four families were. Perhaps not by
the standards to which they had become accustomed in the refugee
hostels, but certainly by our assessment in this country. I noticed that
Marijana had captured the largest Teddy Bear of all for her bed, and Natali
had a wide variety of smaller bears in her section!

We had hardly finished savouring the *Maraška* before the Mansfield
gang arrived, some of them with furrowed brows and darts of hatred in
their eyes when they noticed our presence.

"Just the people we wanted to see!" Mick declared. "P'raps we can all
sit down round a table and sort things out whilst you're here?"

Alan Bull and Malcolm slid quietly out of sight, while Janja led the way
into their dining-room and seated us all round the big table. Meggi and
Big John were there as well, but the children were told to go and watch
television and only two of the mothers attended the meeting.

The main trouble stemmed from a telephone conversation I had had with
the Editor of the Mansfield Chad newspaper the previous day. We had
recently made the unpleasant discovery that someone was visiting our
families once a week with the purpose of collecting money from them,

ostensibly to help pay for their journeys home in May. The same story was confirmed by another Croatian mother who lodged with a local doctor and his wife. Added to this, there had been regular appeals to the general public in the Chad, under the heading "Mercy Mission Fund Appeals for Help"; and people were urged to send as much money as they could spare to certain addresses, or to place their generous donations directly in the Mansfield Branch's account of the Halifax Building Society.

We had promised our families some weeks before that we would be responsible for getting them back home whenever they wished to return; but there was no definite date fixed when they had to leave, now that they would soon be receiving their own passports. We wanted them to feel contented and secure as long as they were our responsibility. They had, as we knew, so many horrors to contemplate which were happening daily in Croatia, and it seemed the least we could do to ease their burdens.

Well, I rang up the Editor of the Chad to explain our intentions, as our families had been lumped together with the remaining twenty-three refugees whenever the demands for money were mentioned. And some of them were beginning to feel very anxious about what was in store for them if they could not find the money – £15 a week was being demanded. The Editor then rang the person concerned to ask a few questions, and clearly he felt that our interference would jeopardize the nice little nest-egg he hoped to accumulate before his journey out to Croatia in May.

"What's the passport situation with the other twenty-three refugees?" Dick asked him. "Have you filled in all the forms and applied for them yet?"

"No point in going to all that trouble," he grunted; "when I've got them all down on my sheet of paper and I'll be taking the whole lot back wi' me in May."

"You won't be taking any of our families," I chipped in. "Some of them are probably going to stay over here and the others haven't made up their minds yet; but we've promised to get them home by air whenever they want to go."

Marica nodded her head emphatically and smiled at me, and the man retreated into a surly silence. But one of the other coach-drivers opened his mouth to excrete a stream of spiteful accusations: we were doing everything in our power to undermine their charitable business, he hissed, and we were trying to poison the minds of our four families against their real friends, who had risked their lives to bring them here from the battle zones. And, furthermore, Dick had had the cheek to check up on the man's own dentist who had done such marvellous work on all the refugees' teeth since they first set foot in England.

This was quite true as we became extremely worried when some of the mothers and their daughters had four or five extractions each, which seemed very sad to us in ones so young. The dentist had eventually proved to be reputable, and the preponderance of bad teeth were probably caused by several years of malnutrition.

Open warfare was at last declared, so I began to accuse the opposing forces of sponging ceaselessly on our families, and of trying to rule their lives and keep them in a state of nervous tension about their futures, while doing nothing to help some of the other poor families who, we understood, were not at all happy in their billets in Mansfield.

Janja hovered in the background, sucking her teeth noisily when she felt I had scored a point; and Meggi made soothing noises from time to time when the whole situation seemed to be getting out of hand. I believe it was Dick, a past master at peaceful negotiations, who finally brought that gritty meeting to a neutral end. Neither side felt they had gained the upper hand, but at least we had all aired our grievances and, we hoped, had helped to protect our families from further inroads into their meagre resources; and quelled some of the worries about what was to happen to them when the coaches returned to Croatia in May.

*　　*　　*　　*　　*　　*

There was a charming man called Eric who worked for a security firm, and who was in charge of the great empty shell of Thoresby House on alternate days. He was not allowed to let anyone into the house unless they had special permission from the Receivers, an invisible body of men who owned the place at that time. But, knowing how much the Croatian families longed to go inside, he risked his job and arranged an appointment for us to meet him at the main gate on the afternoon of January 10th.

I brought with me an old photograph album to show how each room had looked, fully furnished, in the old days. Anica, wearing her smart black coat and shoes, with her emerald-green dress under the coat, took the lead and advanced up the wide staircase into the main hall just behind Eric, while the others followed her exclaiming "*Krasno!* (Wonderful!)" or "*Odlično!* (Great!)" from time to time.

We paused in the big hall to look around, and I showed them a photograph of the Rufford Hunt Ball taking place there some forty years ago. Anica danced around the vast empty space with her eyes half-closed, her arms spread wide and a dreamy expression on her face. Clearly she could picture herself in a beautiful ball-gown dancing with a handsome partner to the music of a Viennese waltz!

Thoresby House and the River Meden in the foreground

"Doesn't it make you feel sad, seeing it all deserted and uncared for like this?" Eric broke in on my thoughts.

"No; not really. You see a house with a hundred and forty-six rooms in it always seemed too big for me to think of as a home," I explained. "The best time of all was when the Army was billeted here during the last war, and the house was full of the sounds of tramping boots, mouth-organs and laughter. After that it became rather sad, with my parents growing older and very few people living in the house or coming to visit us."

Katica and Natali stroked the remains of the faded blue silk material on the drawing-room walls, and Marjan gazed with admiration at the carving of the Queen Oak above the library fireplace, with statues of Robin Hood and Little John on either side of it. We went upstairs to visit our old bedroom – the big wooden shutters and marble mantelpiece were still intact – and many other bedrooms in the west wing; then up and up, till we reached the gymnasium which had windows on all four sides and a wonderful view over the park.

"Look! There's the roof of our home in the Stables," Marijana exclaimed. "You can see all round the world up here, like a bird in the sky."

We opened the trap-door in the tower to show them the flagstaff, and Dragan wanted to climb on to the roof and explore among the chimney-pots, but Eric said "NO! You'll lose me my job, young man, if anyone spots you up there."

After a visit to the huge basement and cellars, we found ourselves out in the garden with four-foot-tall weeds growing up all round us.

"There used to be rose-beds here in the old days," I told them; "and this is the place where Prince Charles had lunch when he came here with the Royal Forestry Society to look at the Thoresby Woods."

"How did he behave? Was he difficult to converse with?" Natali asked.

"No, not at all. He talked about his school days in Scotland, and about the fantastic World Colleges which are of special interest to him, as he hopes to promote friendship and understanding among people from all parts of the world through the pupils who are sent to them. And when it was time for him to leave, he went round thanking every single person who had cooked and served his lunch."

Anica's eyes were round with wonder as she corrected a word here and there, to make sure that the others would fully understand my sketchy Croatian. "Would it not be *odlično* if he paid another visit to this place while we are here? " she sighed.

* * * * * *

Shortly after our visit to Thoresby House, the Social Worker at Skegby Hall who had first noticed the growth on Marica's eyelid phoned to say that she had arranged an appointment for her to see a specialist in Nottingham. We were away when it arrived, so Janet McFerran offered to drive her over to see Mr Malcolm Deane, the eye surgeon. Marica was very nervous, but he told her that it would be an easy operation and she had nothing to worry about. She would probably be able to go home the same night, and would only need to wear a patch over one eye for a short while; and, furthermore, he promised her that it would transform her appearance.

Mr Deane's secretary wrote to us soon afterwards to make the appointment for the operation, and to tell us that the surgeon would like to donate his consultation fee to our fund for helping the Croatian refugees. Everything seemed to be falling into place, apart from Marica herself. She was filled with dark forebodings when I went to the flat to confirm the date of her operation, and she announced that Damir had cried all night when he heard about it. "I'll never see you again, Mummy, if they put you to sleep," he'd sobbed; "because you'll never wake up any more!"

After a further twenty-four hours of wavering, Marica's Balkan upbringing asserted itself. "I cannot possibly make a decision of this nature without my husband's permission," she declared; "so I have written to Zvonko and he will decide."

Some weeks later she received his reply. "The blemish on your eyelid did not deter me when I proposed marriage to you," he wrote; "so there is no reason to suppose that I will stop loving you in the future, if you refuse to undergo this cutting with the knife."

Marica began to smile again, and the dark clouds of anxiety blew away from her face. We telephoned Mr Deane to give him our deepest apologies for wasting his precious time, and life in the Stables settled back into its normal routine; but not until Katica had paid a visit to a local occulist to have her eyes tested.

"What do you think he told me?" she asked us excitedly, while she drew the cork from a bottle of wine she had purchased specially to mark the occasion.

"I've no idea. Did he say he'd order you some nicer frames for your glasses?" I suggested.

"No, no! He said I do not need to wear them any more. Is that not *supair?*"

She poured the wine into six glasses and we all drank a toast to her future without glasses; and suddenly I noticed, for the first time, what pretty blue eyes had been lurking behind those hideous plastic spectacles.

Chapter 9 - Work and Play

February 3rd, 1993, was the date selected for our "Thank You Party". The guests were our neighbours who had given so generously to help furnish the flat and shown kindness to the refugees in many other ways; and from a handful of special friends, the list had now grown to over a hundred people.

We engaged the Kick and Rush Skiffle Group to play during the party, and Cynthia took command of a five-strong working-party consisting of Janja, Katica, Marica, Anica and myself to prepare the food. Innumerable plates of sandwiches, vol-au-vents, cocktail sausages, savoury cheese squares, asparagus tips wrapped in brown bread, angels on horseback and a number of local specialities soon filled the long tables covered with big white Victorian table-cloths, that were placed down the centre of the Pierrepont Gallery.

Janet's boys acted as barmen, while Dragana and Natali (wearing her spectacular black mini-dress) helped pass round the plates of food. The skiffle group

Anica and Cynthia preparing food for the party.

played lively old-fashioned tunes and the women and children danced – apart from Dick, Malcolm, John Orr and Alan Bollans, the men were too shy to venture on to the dance floor. Little Damir took up a position in the middle of the band who had provided him with a primitive wooden instrument to beat; and my five-year-old cousin, Gregor, took up a similar position behind the bar where he helped the McFerran boys dispense the drinks. The stable-yard was filled with the sounds of music and chattering voices, and occasional snatches of song.

Antonija, Anica, Josip and Marjan at the party in the Pierrepont Gallery.

It was a party without regard to mutual interest or class, where some people glared stonily at their neighbours, astonished, perhaps, to find themselves in the same room. But through their midst roamed the fourteen refugees, dressed in their best clothes and only dimly aware of the fierce vibes circulating around the tables laden with food and drink. And yet all those people had kind hearts and generous spirits, or they would not have given so many beautiful things to make a proper home for the families who had lost all their possessions. And, for a little while, they seemed to be part of one huge family, with no divisions or layers of society to keep them in their separate little compartments.

We all joined hands to sing "Auld Lang Syne" at the end of the party. The moon shone serenely in the sky above, and the grey stone buildings glowed with some special magic as the song drifted up through the attic floor to the rafters, where the hay for the horses was stored long ago.

*   *   *   *   *   *

"Could you not find us some outside work to do, *Gospodja*? We have strong arms;" Janja announced, rolling up a sleeve to show me that she spoke the truth. "It would be better for us than sitting all day in the flat doing our *ručni rad* (hand-work) and pondering on the *problemas* back at home."

Their crochet-work was a very beautiful and time-consuming heritage passed down through generations of women in the Balkans. We had received exquisite samples of this from each of the mothers for Christmas, but we knew that it was delicate, exacting work which could be very hard on the eyesight. And there was great sadness when they came face to face with the cheap machine-made table-cloths and tray-cloths made of Nottingham lace, and realized how hard it would be to sell their work for realistic prices.

"Well, there's a field behind our house filled with rubbish and roots of old trees," Dick ventured. "And I'd often thought of keeping a pair of donkeys there if we could get the ground fit for grazing. It would be a tough proposition, but how would you like to tackle something like that?"

"*Supair!*" exclaimed Janja, her eyes glowing with anticipation. "We come at eight o'clock tomorrow morning, O.K.?" She had not bothered to consult the others and we wondered how Anica and Katica, who were built on a much smaller and more delicate scale, would react to this rough man's work.

"Well, we'll just have to see who turns up tomorrow and how they get on," I murmured to Dick. "And I think we should pay them on an hourly rate, at the casual agricultural worker's wage; then it shouldn't cause any aggro in the village?"

Little did I realize the depths of spite and jealousy to which some people will sink!

Promptly at eight o'clock next morning Malcolm's pick-up arrived at the house, and the four women jumped out and grabbed their tools. They were very smartly dressed, their hair swathed in pink or blue woollen snoods worn in the Turkish style, with navy-blue anoraks, dark trousers and wellington boots, provided by the Coal Board. Malcolm had assembled a number of rakes, heavy spades and fierce slashing implements with which to tackle the undergrowth, and he led the way through a small gateway into the field.

"*Nema problema!*" Marica announced, after a few seconds' survey. "We soon make good field for donkeys."

The women dug up old bricks and roots of small trees, slashed the trunks to make them easier to carry, stacked the bricks in a corner of the field and made two large bonfires on which to burn the weeds, branches and roots, and all the other rubbish they found in the field. Malcolm supervised their work, and we had a break at 10.30 each morning when everyone would crowd round the kitchen table to drink coffee, eat cakes and chatter.

Marica and Anica working in the donkey-field.

It only lasted three days, as they worked so hard that the whole field was cleared and raked by the end of that time. But it was a very happy interlude, when the gloom caused by crouching over their crochet-work indoors and watching too much television news was cast aside, and each of the mothers proved that she was capable of doing hard manual work – as well and better than most men would do, Malcolm had to admit.

All the women were desperately keen to earn some extra money to save for their longed-for new homes – if a day should ever dawn when they might dare to dream of such a possibility ... The money they drew from Social Security each week was enough to pay for their food, a few extra clothes for the children and the special twine for their crochet-work. And we had been told they could earn up to £15 a week in casual labour, but anything above that figure would be deducted from their allowances.

Katica's birthday occurred on their last day in the donkey field, so we brought in her birthday cake with thirty-four lighted candles on it during the morning coffee break. Dick danced around the kitchen brandishing a sharp carving-knife, Anica and Marica shrieked with excitement, and Cynthia and I placed a few parcels around Katica's plate. We found half a bottle of *šljivovic* in the larder and poured out a small glass for everyone, while Dick led the singing of "Happy birthday ..."

"I wish we could make every day like the last three," Janja said. "Have you no more fields that need some work doing in them?"

Malcolm thought for a little while, then suggested the churchyard; it was very overgrown round the edges, he told us, and badly needed weeding and trimming. It was agreed that the mothers would start work over there the following Monday; and that was when their beautiful interlude came to a sudden end.

"What are those bleeding foreign women doing, earning money in our village when they haven't even got work permits and are drawing God knows how much on the dole each week? Better ring up Social Security in Mansfield and tell 'em what's goin' on!"

The people who uttered those words were too cowardly to come to us in person and speak their minds. Also too lazy to volunteer for such hard work themselves. I had never realized before the arrival of the refugees that so many stones had verminous insects lurking beneath them.

* * * * * *

The children, meanwhile, were getting on well at school. There were no complaints about the new coach-driver who fetched and brought them home each day, and Mr Warley had certainly spoken some magic words in the class-room where Dragana and Natali worked, as there were no more tears shed nor tales of nastiness from their class-mates when they returned to the flat.

A dance was held in the village hall on February 14th to celebrate St Valentine's Day and Malcolm, who was Chairman of the Perlethorpe Social Club that year, invited the Croatians to come to it. I am not sure how many accepted his invitation, but I know that Marijana was one of the group.

Each time we saw her in the flat, she was vacuuming the carpet down the long corridor, washing dishes in the kitchen sink or struggling with the homework she brought back from college, a rather sombre expression on her face and a hint of sadness about the eyes. Unlike Dragana and Natali, she found it very hard to learn English, and she had no special friends to confide in at home as she was four years older than any of the other children; but she had such a sweet nature that I longed to see her smile.

Marijana's lucky star was shining on that cold and frosty night in February. Half way through the evening a handsome dark-haired lad called Robert came across and invited her to dance. They had met briefly on one or two previous occasions as they were originally introduced by Malcolm and Cynthia at the New Year's Eve party. It was, however, a bold move on the part of Robert to cross the hall and ask her to dance, with the eyes of Perlethorpe village boring into his back.

Their dance was clearly a success, although they were hardly able to exchange a word with each other; but it did not matter for it led to further dances, then Robert called at the Stables' flat and made a date with her for the following Saturday. The Croatian mothers thought it prudent to send another girl or two to accompany Marijana on that first occasion. Poor Robert and Marijana, with a pair of giggling teenagers trotting along a few yards behind them, wherever they went! It must have been an agonizing date, but it did not deter them.

We were in London at the time, but Marica pulled me into their bedroom as soon as we returned, to tell me everything that had happened during our absence.

"Marijana is besotted with this boy," she confided in a hoarse whisper; "and she no longer sleeps at night for thinking of him. Tell me all you know about him, *Gospodja*?"

"Well, he comes of a very nice family who live in the village of Budby at the far end of the lake, and his father has worked on the estate for a good many years. Robert used to come to the children's club in Perlethorpe when we first started it, and he always seemed an intelligent well-mannered boy. But I don't know him all that well, you understand?"

Marijana had joined us in the bedroom by that time and she pleaded, "Could you not have a talk with him yourself to find out what his intentions are? I mean whether he really likes me, or just wants to have many different girl-friends – perhaps a new one each month?"

Very foolishly I caved in and said I would do my best for the poor girl. I selected the Pierrepont Gallery as neutral ground, and asked Robert to meet me there the following afternoon.

It proved, when the time came, to be the most embarrassing interview I had ever taken part in. Robert was no longer a lively teenager showing off his new motor-bike – that was how I remembered him – but a serious young man with a job and a future to consider. We met in the gallery with Mother's paintings all around us, regarding us with mocking eyes. I offered him a seat on the four-sided *conversazione* while I sat down in a large Gainsborough chair some distance away from him. There was, unfortunately, no cosy arrangement of chairs grouped together, but I had purposely left the lights switched off so that the gallery was only lit by the wintry afternoon greyness filtering through some windows, high up.

Well, here we go, I thought to myself; who's going to take the first plunge? I can't very well say "What are your intentions towards this girl whom you invited to dance with you at the St Valentine's dance two weeks ago?"

Robert, meanwhile, preserved a sepulchral silence, while he regarded some imperfection on the toe of his right shoe with intense interest.

"I hear there was a good party at the village hall on the 14th," I ventured at last. "Wish we'd been able to go to it too."

A grunt came from the *conversazione* , then we relapsed into a further pool of silence.

"Have you ever been to Jugoslavia?" I tried again.

He raised his eyes briefly and looked at me as if I'd asked if he'd ever been inside a brothel, then he replied; "No, I've never been out of England and only once as far as Skegness."

For some unknown reason, this last remark made me feel quite talkative; so I chattered about some of our holidays in Croatia and what an old-fashioned country it was, and how men took first place there while the women mostly stayed at home and did what they were told – a glimmer of a smile illuminated my victim's face. I touched on the strictness of parental discipline, and how the children really had to obey their elders, quite unlike what happened in England – we both smirked at each other briefly – and, finally, I produced my master-stroke:

"I took one or two photos to finish up my film the other day and I think these two have come out rather well. Would you like to have one of them?"

I handed him a couple of pictures of Marijana, Ivana and Damir out for a walk near the Stables, with the trees and grass covered in a white frost and the children holding hands and smiling happily. He studied them intently for a few minutes, then said; "I think I'd like this one if you can spare it, please, 'cos it's got Dosco in the picture – just there on the left."

I handed it to him and would have liked to shout, "What the hell's our dog got to do with a photo of your girl-friend?"

But I bit my tongue instead, and we both rose to our feet and sped thankfully towards the door of the gallery.

*   *   *   *   *   *

The Antiques Fair came to Thoresby on March 6th, and our four mothers were offered a stand in the Old Riding School where they could display some of their crochet-work. Anica and Marica sat on one side of a large table with Janja and Katica opposite them, each one crocheting away for dear life but, simultaneously, keeping a sharp eye open for any potential customers. Many people showed interest and paused to watch them working, but there were only a few purchasers.

Anica and Marica showing their crochet-work and embroidery at the Thoresby Antique Fair in March 1993.

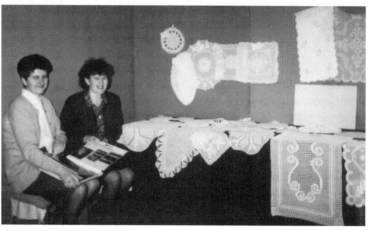

Janja and Katica with some of their work.

Marica secured one or two orders for future work, among them a dressing-table cloth for Ranji, the wife of my cousin, Hugh, to be made to her own special measurements. Janja and Katica looked rather jealous when this occurred and, for the first time, it slowly dawned on us that being cooped up together in such a confined space was not exactly a breeding-ground for sisterly love.

"Imagine sharing that tiny kitchen with three other women," I said to Dick, who replied that he thought it might be no worse than sharing one with a 10-stone Newfoundland dog!

Further proof of a mini-Balkan conflagration in the refugees' flat blew up when their quarterly telephone bill arrived. It was about £750, and we brought it along to show them to have a serious discussion about the future use of the telephone. Anica and Marica threw up their hands in horror once they had absorbed the size of the bill, and they assured us that they always cycled to the call-box on the main road near Perlethorpe village when they wished to ring their families back in Croatia. We knew this to be true, but were not prepared for the angry exchanges in rapid Croatian which then took place between the four women.

"Tear the telephone from the wall and remove it out of harm's way," Marica advised us, her arms flailing the air angrily. "As long as it remains here, promises will be broken and the next time you will have a bill of one thousands pounds, I swear to you!"

Her recriminatory eyes darted to and fro, like magnets seeking a solid lump of iron on which to fasten. Luckily Janet came to the rescue by finding some marvellous device that you could clamp on to the telephone; it allowed you to receive incoming calls and make local outgoing ones, but nothing beyond a five mile radius. This seemed a fair compromise to which everyone agreed – some more willingly than others.

*   *   *   *   *   *

Our old friend, Jean Melhuish from St Margaret's Bay, came to visit us at the end of the month, and she was very anxious to renew her brief acquaintanceship with the mothers and children. We took her to have special Croatian coffee and cakes in the Stables' flat, then played ball games with the children on the hill outside their home and took them all to visit the waterfalls down by the lake. Later that evening we went to a dance in the village hall and watched Robert and Marijana gazing into each others eyes while they danced together.

Natali's fifteenth birthday occurred on April 1st. We had a big tea-party at home that day, followed by games for the children out in the garden; and Antonija played Grandpa's piano for the first time – quite beautifully.

"Yes, she is very musical," Anica confided proudly. "She used to sing at children's concerts in Zagreb before the war started."

Antonija blushed furiously and hid her face behind her amazing crop of brownish-gold hair. She was learning English very fast, unlike her brother Marjan, and she had many friends at school and a few admirers among the village lads.

Rowan asked us next morning if we knew that there was a free cottage at the bottom of our garden. "It's just been done up and repainted, and there's a new family arriving here next week to work on the site of Hugh's house who might move in there, unless you had thought seriously about splitting up the fourteen women and children in the Stables?"

"They've all decided to stay here now, and not return to their own country in Mick's coach in May, so we'd better ask them if they'd like more space before you let the cottage go," Dick replied.

He broached the subject with Janja that afternoon, and she replied immediately, "We go see this house now, O.K.?"

She and Katica fetched their jackets and scarves, and we drove them to No. 3, Meadow Cottages, very close to Perlethorpe Post Office. It is a red brick Victorian cottage with a small front garden and a large back one which had been neglected for many years. There were three small bedrooms and a bathroom upstairs, and a kitchen and big sitting-room downstairs, with a shed full of rubbish out at the back.

The two women went swiftly into each room, opened and shut the doors of all the fitted cupboards, then tramped through the nettles and weeds to the far end of the garden and back.

"We like!" Janja announced on their return. "We move in tomorrow, O.K.?"

"They certainly didn't take long to make up their minds," I whispered to Dick. "But we'll have to get them a cooker and fridge and some curtains and carpets, etc., before we can move them from the Stables."

"You move after three days," Dick pronounced each word carefully. "First we make your house ready, O.K.?"

All the Croatians were delighted about the move, and Marica and Anica became good friends with the other two mothers again, once they had left the flat and a certain amount of bickering about which pieces of furniture they should take with them had subsided.

After the school bus had called at both addresses and removed all the children, two of the mothers would set off on foot or on their bicycles to visit the other pair and take coffee and sweet cakes with them – one day at Meadow Cottages and the next day at the Stables' flat.

Katica invited us to have lunch in their new home, of which they were intensely proud. Janja, who was stirring a large tureen of soup when we arrived, turned round and said; "You have brought peace into our lives, instead of war. They should send you to Bosnia to arrange matters out there!"

Chapter 10 - Big John

The Nottingham Evening Post published an article about the middle of April entitled "Photograph of Hope". There was a picture of Ivana standing in front of Thoresby House holding a photograph of her father reading the Nottingham Evening Post in Croatia, and the narrative ran as follows:

"The last time Zvonko Ðerd saw his eleven-year-old daughter, Ivana, was in their Croatian homeland almost a year ago. She was one of the lucky ones. As the Serbian forces closed in on her home town of Ilok, near Vukovar, Ivana, along with her brother, sister and mother escaped to Britain, and the safety of Thoresby Hall near Mansfield.

"They were part of a group of 37 refugees brought out of the country by Notts coach operator, Mick Gelsthorpe, owner of Janick Travel, and his drivers. Ivana featured on the front page of the Evening Post's Christmas Eve edition, wishing for peace in her homeland and a call from her father.

"Thanks to one of the drivers, Zvonko saw for himself that his daughter was safe and well. He took a copy of the paper along to the coastal town of Opatija where Zvonko was awaiting treatment for wounds he received in the fighting. 'At first he did not recognise her,' the man said; 'but when he saw it was Ivana he was overcome.'

"When he last saw her Ivana had been a terrified little girl caught in the middle of events she did not understand and could not control.

'She was so frightened she just sat in a corner. It was four hours before I could get her to speak,' said the driver. 'Now she's a different girl altogether, so happy and will run up and put her arms around me.'

"The two men have now become firm friends and see each other every time he is in the area on a mercy mission. The next trip will be next month when 14 of the 37 refugees will be going home – but Ivana and her family will not be among them. Their home has been razed to the ground and their town is occupied. They have nowhere to go. But the family may soon be reunited in this country.

"Zvonko is now seeking the papers which will allow him to come to Britain to be with his family again. In the meantime there are letters, telephone calls and the hope that they will all be together again soon.

"Funds are still needed for the £2,000 it takes for every mercy mission, and donations can be made on Mansfield xxxxxx."

It seemed a touching little story on the face of it, but it caused an uproar in the Stables' flat. And Marica finally put her foot down and forbade that driver to enter her home, ever again.

"What a good thing!" we both exclaimed when we heard the news. We've been trying to get rid of him for months and now, at last, he's cooked his own goose."

Marica told us that he had come to Thoresby with two newspapermen and got hold of Ivana without her knowledge, then made her pose in front of Thoresby House holding up a photograph of her father (which she, Marica herself, had never seen before). Many things in the article were dirty lies, she declared; just take a look at the last sentence, for example ... That alone proved that he was merely using her Ivana to get money for his own evil purposes!

She became so upset about the whole business that we promised to ring up the Editor and point out the inaccuracies told to his reporter by that driver, and ask for an apology.

Big John was now the only one left of the original trio, who was always welcome in either of the Croatian family's homes. All the children loved him and he hardly ever came to see them empty-handed: one day he would bring a new football for the boys, another day a television game for the girls; then there were expeditions in his car to skating-rinks, swimming-pools and, most exciting of all, to *tae-kwondo* classes in Mansfield. The mothers were not too keen on the idea at first as it involved them in the expense of buying special costumes for the contestants to wear; but when the children began to plead with tears in their eyes, it was no longer possible to deny them. Dragan, Ivan, Josip and Ivana were the first ones to strive for their Green Belts; but, later on, little Damir was allowed to join them and brought home a silver trophy one proud day!

John was not always around, as he would sometimes return to Croatia for a month or two to work as a volunteer with a reconstruction unit who were trying to rebuild orphanages and children's homes which had been destroyed by the Serbs. He wrote to us occasionally while he was abroad, and he had a way of describing some of the horrors among which he chose to live that brought them very close to us.

Back in England, during one of his visits to Thoresby, Big John told us about an incident that had taken place in Pakrac the previous month. It was a town on the frontier line between Serbia and Croatia, where the atmosphere was always very tense.

"I was sitting in this café having a beer when a drunk policeman – one of the Ustaže I think he was – came and sat down at my table. He had mad, blank sort of eyes, know what I mean, and he held a loaded gun which he kept pointing at my stomach across the table. He was a giant of a man who'd been in a Serbian prison-camp before, and he kept saying to me; 'U.N. bastards no good! You drink! You drink!' – and waving that awful gun around only three feet away from me.

"He fell off his chair at one point, still clasping his gun; then he opened it, took out fifteen bullets and gave them to me to hold.

'This is better,' I thought to myself. 'He must trust me or he wouldn't give me his bullets.' But the next moment

Big John in Pakrac.

he asked for them back, and that was when I began to feel really frightened.

"After a long while I made my getaway, but my hands were shaking so much that I could hardly fit the key into the lock on the door of the car. My mates were really pleased to see me back safe, I can tell you!

"The police, you understand, are the most dangerous people out there at present. They've had no proper training, and most of them suffered terrible things in the camps; and they're all armed to the teeth ... they're like crazy wild animals."

*   *   *   *   *   *

We were back in London when Rowan rang up from the estate office one day and said; "I've just had a call from someone I know in Mansfield."

"Oh, yes? And what did he want?"

"It's about Big John. Apparently they'd discovered that he spends a lot of his time over at Thoresby nowadays, and they say we're to watch out as he's had a bit of a chequered career in the past!"

"What sort of things has he done?" I asked anxiously, thinking of all those innocent children going off to skating-rinks and swimming-pools with him.

"Well, I don't want to go into details, but I believe he can be quite aggressive at times, and he's a tricky customer to deal with."

"Thanks for warning us," I said; "we'll bear it in mind."

It was a difficult situation because everyone liked Big John, and the children would be devastated if they were not allowed to see him any more. We decided in the end that it would be best to drop a hint of what we had heard to the mothers, to see how they would react to it.

"*Veliki* John, O.K.!" Janja stressed, after she had heard the news. "John good man. We like him, children like him, No *problema*."

"John good man!" chimed the other mothers. "Maybe looks tough, but his heart is warm."

"O.K., no *problema*," we agreed. "But we'll keep our eyes open, understand?"

But the more we kept our eyes open, the more convinced we became that the refugee children, both here in England and back in their own country, were being the salvation of Big John.We knew that he had children of his own, and even some grandchildren, at home in Mansfield; and that he always wore a rough woollen pullover and ancient knitted cap on his head, and only shaved occasionally. And that Bobby, the nurse who went to Croatia with the coaches last November, had described him as "driftwood" and implied that he was a good-for-nothing layabout.

John told us later that he had been very hurt with the way he was treated by some of the others during that journey. They asked him not to accompany them on their search for the refugee families because his appearance, they said, would frighten the children and make everything harder for them to arrange.

"But when we got started on the journey home, it was me the kids came to," he told us; "and me who played games with them and kept them smiling all the way back to England."

Shortly before he returned to Croatia that summer he brought us some poems to read, written by an orphan girl called Emira from Pakrac, whose parents were murdered in the ethnic cleansing near Banja Luka the previous year. They were written with great depth of feeling – images of misery and bitterness which were very sad to read from the pen of such a young girl.

But hidden among them I found two unsigned poems that seemed even more moving than any of the others I had read. This is one of them:-

SHOT IN CHILDHOOD

Our house has a roof of moonlight,
And my first nights of sleep were broken,
But there is still an echo of the first spoken word,
And the drawing on the wall.
"Mama, tell me, Mama;
What kind of man can put his eye to the sight,
And shoot at a little girl with a doll?
Tell him, Mama,
There was sunlight, there was laughter,
And fields of flowers,
There was a sunrise, and a mountain,
And our church had bells;
Tell him, Mama,
That I have made a roof of dreams,
And that in my dreams I may even ...
FORGIVE HIM."

"That's quite a different style to Emira's poems; surely she didn't write that one, did she?" I looked hard at John, but he had found something particularly interesting to gaze at on the far side of the room. A dark purple flush appeared on his face, rising slowly upwards from the neck.

And then I knew – and another unsuspected glimpse of Big John was revealed to us.

Chapter 11 - London Interludes

A coach drew up outside our house in Narrow Street on the 6th of April, and a large party of adults and children scrambled out on to the pavement. First there was little Damir who gave me a full frontal, closely followed by twenty-six more kisses from thirteen other passengers – by the time Dick and I had clocked up fifty-four kisses between us, the Limehouse natives had bulgy eyeballs and open mouths.

After all the Croatians had landed safely on London soil, Malcolm and Cynthia emerged from the back of the coach and, finally, the pair of Nottinghamshire coach-drivers. They glanced around them with suspicious eyes, then sprinted rapidly across the road into Booty's Wine Bar where we had booked lunch for the whole party.

Booty's used to be the engine repair shop for Woodward Fisher's Barge Yard when we first came to Limehouse some twenty-five years ago. A narrow primeval house on the waterfront, dipping its back legs into the river at high tide, it lost none of its magic when Dennis Booty and his wife, Maureen, transformed it into a flourishing wine bar after the demise of the old barge yard. Dennis had been a well-known boxer in his youth, and his wife was a big woman with blue eyes, a broad smiling face and a warm and cheerful personality to match her looks.

She had taken immense trouble to compose a menu that she thought would appeal to 'those poor little starving mites', as she referred to our Croatian children.

Maureen Booty.

We had chicken soup, home-made shepherd's pie and peas, followed by apple tart and cream; and Maureen had reserved all the best tables nearest to the windows for us, so that our guests could admire the river and the ships steaming by. But the trouble was that some of our big family were still feeling sick after their long journey to London, while others were tired and rather frightened by the teeming city in which they found themselves. And the biggest problem of all was that they just do not like our English cooking. The mothers resolutely finished everything on their plates, but some of the children only pecked at theirs.

Malcolm, Cynthia and the coach-drivers, on the other hand, ate well enough to bring gladness to Maureen's heart. But each time one of them made eye contact with a local drinking at the bar, I sensed a ripple of mutual distrust passing through the ether.

"I think it's going to be a difficult afternoon," Dick muttered pessimistically in my right ear as we stood up to leave.

After a guided tour of our house, we emerged on to the pavement again just as Debbie Owen was getting out of her car. She came across to greet our party – she had often heard about them during the past six months – and told them that her husband was even then in Sarajevo, striving for a peaceful settlement with the Serbs. I am not sure how much our mothers understood but it was, perhaps, an important landmark in their day – something to mention in their next letters home.

Dick and I joined the party in the coach for a visit to the Tower of London. The driver dropped us on the south side of Tower Bridge and, pointing to a coach-parking area on our right, he called out to us; "See you there in about two hours' time?"

Katica and Janja and their children enjoyed crossing Tower Bridge. There was H.M.S. BELFAST and the Tower of London to look at on one side, and all the tugs and river-launches surging by under the bridge, and crowds of foreign tourists jostling each other to lean over the parapet and watch the swirling river far below. A fresh west wind was blowing that day, and Antonija's hair blew out like a shimmering gold rug while we paused to take photographs of all our party near the entrance to the Tower. Once inside, our visit was a mixed success. In the first place, there were far too many people, whichever way you looked; and the queue to see the Queen's Crown Jewels was so long and slow-moving that we gave up trying after a while. We wandered around disconsolately, gazing at the chopping-block where various famous people had parted company with their heads, and at the Raven Master feeding his ravens; then Dick saw a very small queue outside the Armoury and, because he has always loved old guns and swords, etc., he said; "Let's go in there!"

Dragan, Ivan, Josip and Marjan were very pleased with his choice, so the rest of us tagged along behind them; but it was not until we reached a glass case filled with blunderbusses that Marijana touched my arm and said that she wanted to ask me some questions about Robert – in private. We let everyone else drift past us, then she released what was on her mind in rapid Croatian – like a racing-car revving up before the starting-flag descends.

I understood very little of what she was saying, but formed a general impression that she was worried and upset by the lack of visible progress in her relationship with her English boy-friend, although they met nearly every day. What should she do to discover his intentions, she demanded?

I gazed at the blunderbusses for inspiration, but they looked back at me with blank cold eyes. *"Polako! polako!* (Go slowly! go slowly!)" I suggested. "Do not be impatient, but drop a hint about another boy-friend at your college, and make him jealous; then you will see things move much faster!"

"Oh, that I could not do. It would not be truthful!" She looked horrified; but I noticed a shadow of thoughtfulness pass across her face.

"Where on earth have you been?" Dick's voice bellowed up the stairs. "We've been hunting everywhere for you."

"Coming!" I shouted back, quite relieved that I need not offer any more doubtful advice – for the time being, at any rate.

We hurried back across Tower Bridge as we were a few minutes late for our rendezvous with the coach; but when we reached the big coach-park there were coaches from Spain, Germany, Sweden, Luxembourg, France, Devonshire, Birmingham and Liverpool, but not a glimpse of our Nottinghamshire coach which had "Spencers of Mansfield" written in large green letters across the back of it.

"Don't tell me they've gone to some other car-park and we'll never see them again!" Cynthia released a cavernous sigh.

"Well, we'll have to go and ask the man in the little box down there, then start searching," I said, trying to sound cheerful and optimistic.

"I've bin sittin' 'ere all day, doll, and they ain't gorn past this barrier 'cos there weren't no room for 'em, see?"

"Yes, I see what you mean." I felt like bursting into tears as I had just caught sight of some of the children's faces – tired, bewildered and rather scared they looked.

Dick came to the rescue and drew up a plan of action. "You go towards Tower Bridge and stand on the corner up there," he directed; "and we'll get Malcolm to patrol along Tooley Street while I go further afield to the car-park behind Guy's Hospital. And you, Cynthia, had better stay here and keep everyone smiling!"

We set off in our various directions, but returned after half-an-hour with no results. By that time the Croatians were sitting around on walls and the edge of the pavement, looking utterly forlorn.

"We'll give them another fifteen minutes, then we'll have to take you on the underground to King's Cross and put you on a train to Retford, if the coach is still missing," Dick predicted. It was very difficult to know what to suggest for such a large party who had already had their fill of London.

I returned to my corner of Tower Bridge Road and Queen Elizabeth Street, without any real hope of ever seeing that vile coach again. I glanced at my watch every two minutes, and some twelve and a half minutes later I was about to leave my watch-position for the last time when a familiar voice called out; "Joomp in, loov! We was joost havin' a look round to see where our party were hidin' itself."

The coach driver said they had been parked all the time in Jamaica Road, on the far side of Tower Bridge Road, because they couldn't find any room in the big coach-park; and they were also becoming a little worried about the loss of their passengers, I was glad to be told!

We went to Covent Garden for the final treat, before Spencers' coach set off back to Nottinghamshire. That was the best part of the whole outing the children said, when we asked them about it later on. We ordered coffee, Coca Cola, cakes and ice creams at an outdoor café; and there was music and jugglers, and many little shops and market stalls for buying souvenirs for their friends at school.

Dick and I stood on the pavement to wave the travellers goodbye. I was clutching a basket of daffodils – a present from our big family – as Spencers' coach swept past us; and all that was left was a bunch of waving hands and a belch of smoke as the coach was swallowed up in the evening rush-hour.

*   *   *   *   *   *

We all had a lovely time celebrating Damir's seventh birthday. It was the First of May with a deep blue sky and golden sunbeams filtering through the young green leaves all over Sherwood Forest. Dick borrowed the large Land Rover belonging to the Home Farm to drive us – all sixteen of us – to the fun-fair near Edwinstowe.

Some of us started with a ride in the ghost-train, while others made straight for the bumper-cars which were so popular that it was hard to drag the children away from them. Later we killed lions and tigers at the shooting-range, sampled a peaceful little roundabout and faced unimaginable horrors racing each other down the tall helter-skelter; it

Damir on the railings in front of Thoresby House. Spring 1993.

Natali and Dragana on the ghost train at the fair at Edwinstowe.

caused Damir to shriek with excitement while his mother appealed to the Virgin Mary for his protection.

Janja, Ivana and Josip posed for their photographs with their faces looking out from the bodies of Robin Hood, Maid Marion and Friar Tuck. Then we drove back to Butterfields and played football in the garden till all the grown-ups were tired and thirsty. At that moment I emerged from the kitchen carrying Damir's chocolate birthday cake with seven lighted candles flickering in the breeze, while Anica and Marica poured out tea or Coca Cola for everyone there. Damir blew out his candles with one big puff, and we all sang "Happy Birthday" and gathered round to watch him open his parcels.

After a few months I had noticed one rather curious feature about the children's birthdays. They would open their parcels with great delight on the big day, then semi-rewrap them soon afterwards, so that they could produce them a number of times in the future and share the pleasure of opening them all over again with some visitors who came to the flat. I often wondered how long they must wait before the contents of those parcels would finally shed their wrappings and be put into use or play!

A few days after Damir's birthday, the Mansfield Chad printed an article entitled "CROATIANS LEAVE AFTER VISA HITCH – Euro-MP steps in to sort out tense situation."

Mick Gelsthorpe was planning to take sixteen of the original group of thirty-seven refugees back to Croatia in May, but the Belgian Immigration Authorities had refused them transit visas at the last moment. Because they had no passports and the only record of them entering England was contained on the one sheet of paper, they were unable to travel by air as individual families. This caused much irritation to Mick and his drivers who were only too anxious to get rid of them now that the six months had come to an end. But Ken Coates, the Euro-MP, came to their rescue by appealing to the Belgian Embassy in London, so they were finally able to leave England at the beginning of June.

"Are you sorry you are not going back with them?" Dick asked Janja, the day we read about them in the Chad.

There was a chorus of "Noes" from the four mothers, and Janja added forcefully; "We ask you when we want to go home. No go by coach with Mick or his driver, you promise?"

"Well, we hope you'll stay here, perhaps for years and years," I said in my best Croatian. "And we hope some of your husbands will be able to come and visit you one day soon."

*   *   *   *   *   *

Dick had written four letters during the early spring, one for each mother to send to her husband in Croatia inviting him to come to England for a month's holiday, to be spent with us at Thoresby, whenever he could make arrangements to leave his country. These letters were essential, we had been told, for the men to show to the Immigration Authorities when they first arrived in England, together with our presence at the airport to prove that they were genuine.

We had forgotten all about them till Anica phoned us in London one morning to announce; "My husband arrive Saturday, Croatia Airlines, at 11.30 a.m. Heathrow. Please, will you meet him?"

I hastily glanced through our diary, then told her we could meet him but not bring him straight back to Thoresby. He would have to spend the night with us in London as we had an important engagement next morning, but we could drive him north with us as early as possible that afternoon. We spoke to Cynthia on the telephone later on, to ask how everyone else was taking the news.

"Janja and Katica are bloody furious!" she told us. "They've been on the phone to their husbands to try and get them booked on planes a week later, as far as I can gather. But Marica is taking it quite calmly. She says her husband is not well enough to travel yet, but she hopes he'll come for Christmas instead."

Dick, Dosco and I set off early on Saturday morning and drove into London Airport about 10.30 a.m. We took Dosco for a walk round some very neat flower-beds planted outside Terminal 2's car-park, then we left him in the car and reached the Arrival Hall with half an hour to spare.

"Yes, Flight 401 from Zagreb is expected to land on time," the girl at the Croatian Airways desk confirmed. "If you care to wait near the passenger's exit along at the far end of the hall, you will be sure to meet your friend there soon after midday."

We had a quick cup of coffee and a cheese sandwich each, and as soon as the landing of the plane from Zagreb was announced on the big notice-board, I ran to a telephone to tell Anica. I could feel waves of excitement rushing down the line, and the sound of children's voices asking questions excitedly in the background.

"I'll ring you again the moment he comes through that door, then you can all speak to him yourselves! Must run now as a few passengers are just beginning to appear," I told her.

"How shall we know which one he is?" I asked Dick, as we scanned the crowd coming through the barrier – faster and denser each minute.

A chauffeur holding up a board to attract some unknown person's attention was standing next to me, and he told me that a plane from Tel Aviv had touched down about the same time as the Croatian one. There were men wearing black berets with dark bushy eyebrows and broad Slav cheek-bones shouldering their way through the crowd; women with bleached hair and the latest Italian designer-wear clothes; a striking auburn head which rose imperiously above the lesser mortals around it; a pair of spoilt children accompanied by their Yiddisher mama, swathed in pearls; and a surge of men with black beards thrust out in front of them like the fuzzy microphones employed by reporters on the track of a good story.

But there was no one who looked quite like Anica's description of her Anton.

A voice summoned Dick over the loudspeaker system at that moment. "Will Dr Raynes please come to the information desk immediately."

A ripple of excitement tinged with worry flitted through my brain as we hurried across the hall to the big central office.

"Yes, Mr Hržić has landed safely from Zagreb," the girl told us; "but they're keeping him in Immigration for an interview, and as he doesn't speak any English this may take some while. Would you, therefore, mind waiting in the little room next to the Arrivals gateway, and someone will contact you there when they've finished with him."

"Couldn't I act as interpreter?" I asked, "I can understand the language well enough to translate any questions and answers."

The girl looked doubtful, but said she would ask Immigration and let us know.

It was just after midday when we joined a small crowd of timid-eyed foreigners in the waiting-room and sat down on the two remaining chairs. There was a couple from Bangladesh with their daughter, a pair of Turkish Cypriots and a group of West Indians. One of the men whistled a catchy tune while his girl-friend wiggled her hips and beat a steady tattoo on the floor with the toes of her shoes.

A female Immigration Officer paid us a visit after half an hour, and said she regretted the interpreter had gone to lunch and wouldn't be back before two at the earliest.

"Surely I could translate for them, couldn't I? I know the language pretty well," I boasted.

"Oh no, that wouldn't do at all!" The woman gave me a stern look. "How are we to know that you would be telling the truth?"

"Because there's no point in me making up a pack of lies when there's nothing to lie about," I replied angrily. "This man has three weeks' leave from the army to visit his family who've been with us for the past eight months – they came to England as political refugees last November. I don't see what the problem is? He has a letter from us inviting him to stay, and he's unlikely to outstay his leave or he'd become a deserter in the Croatian army."

"I'll tell the Officer-in-Charge what you say, but nothing is likely to happen till after lunch now."

Dick and I returned to the car and took Dosco for a walk round and round the flower-beds near Terminal 2, and gave him a bowl of water and some biscuits to eat. Afterwards we plodded back to Arrivals and phoned Anica to tell her what was happening, then ordered fish and chips in the cafeteria and read the morning papers.

We were back in the waiting-room punctually at two o'clock, and finally left there at 6.30 p.m., still without a glimpse of Anton. Every hour a junior Immigration Officer looked in to see if we were still there and to tell us, firstly, that the interpreter had not yet finished her lunch; secondly, that she had arrived, but did not think this man was giving satisfactory answers or telling the truth about how long he intended to stay here; and, thirdly, that they were considering putting him on the next flight back to Zagreb.

Dick had become exceedingly angry by that time. An Indian solicitor came into the waiting-room to help one of his clients, and when he proffered his business card we accepted it with pleasure, thinking his services might soon be required. Dick then demanded to see the Head Duty Officer, after dropping a hint about Lord Owen being a neighbour and old friend of ours.

An hour or so later, we strode past the barrier and into the Immigration Hall ourselves. The man behind the desk said he had not yet been able to contact the Head Duty Officer who was extremely busy that afternoon; but the return plane to Zagreb had already left and, as they had no spare sleeping accommodation available for illegal immigrants, they might consider releasing Anton to us for one night only. But we would have to wait until the Head Duty Officer was free to discuss the matter in person; and give him our word that we would bring Mr Hržić Anton back to Heathrow first thing tomorrow morning.

"And what makes you so sure that he won't escape overnight, after receiving this appalling treatment on arrival in England?" Dick asked the man, who shrivelled inside his jacket when he observed the look in my husband's eye. "You have implied that he and I (who wrote the letter inviting him here) are no better than common liars, so I shall now drive straight back home. This is my telephone number, if your Duty Officer can finally spare a moment to speak to me after wasting seven hours of my valuable time sitting around in this despicable place."

We drove disconsolately back home, and I kept thinking of poor Anton imprisoned in some little cell at Heathrow with no one to talk to, no chance of seeing his family after all those months apart and facing the threat of being flown back to Croatia first thing tomorrow morning.

I could hear the telephone ringing as Dick turned the key in our front door lock. I rushed inside and grabbed the instrument, and a silky voice at the other end of the line announced that he was the Duty Officer at Heathrow, Terminal 2, and he would like to have a word with Dr Raynes if it was convenient?

"You can come back and fetch Mr Hržić now, or we'll send him over to you in a taxi, " the man informed Dick. "We've decided to entrust him into your care for the next three weeks after all!"

The journey from Heathrow across London to our house takes over an hour, sometimes two, depending on the traffic.

"Put him into a taxi, will you, and I shall be writing to the Home Office to demand an explanation of your monstrous treatment of a visitor arriving in this country for the first time." Dick slammed the phone down and I started cooking a big supper for Anton – imagining that he would be very hungry when he finally arrived.

Some weeks later we heard from a judge who had many dealings with the Immigration Service at London Airport that they were in the habit of employing Serbian interpreters there, without realizing the difference. And the one they used in Anton's case had altered most of his answers to the Immigration Officers' questions, in order to portray him as an untrustworthy villain who should on no account be allowed to stay in this country.

Poor Anton was very upset, bewildered and dog-tired by the time he stepped out of his taxi in front of 88, Narrow Street. He was an ambulance-driver who had been conscripted into the Croatian army the previous year, and was working just behind the front line most of the time. He had never left his own country nor flown in an aeroplane before; and he was far too exhausted to eat much supper that evening, but Dick opened a bottle of Lutomer Reisling, a favourite Croatian wine of ours, while I dialled Anica's number. His sad brown eyes filled with joy at last, and after a long conversation with all his family he unpacked his small holdall and presented us with two carefully chosen presents from Croatia.

*   *   *   *   *   *

The old Regent Canal Dock renamed Limehouse Basin, was due to be reopened next morning after four years' closure due to the building of the Limehouse Link Road. Dick and I had been invited to the opening ceremony aboard the P.L.A. Vessel *NORE,* and we asked Anton if he would like to come along with us after assuring him that it would not last long and we would soon be on our way up north, to take him to his waiting family.

I suffered a few misgivings as we approached the *NORE* which was filled with local dignitaries happily swilling pints of beer. There had been no chance to ask if we might bring a guest, but Anton received a warm welcome aboard and a glass was quickly pressed into his hands. The ropes were cast off and we motored round and round Limehouse Basin watching the gaily painted narrow-boats, the small tugs, sailing-craft and canoes, all taking part in the fun. After a while the *NORE* returned to her berth near the lock-gates, and the Port of London Authority Chief stood up to make a speech. He dwelt at some length on the re-opening of the dock and what it would mean to the people of Limehouse and the narrow-boat owners traversing England via the River Thames and the Regent Canal; then he gave a special welcome to Anton and said, on behalf of all those present, that they had watched the war scenes in his country on television news with deep horror and sadness, and they wished him joy during his short visit to England and would like to present him with a plaque which represented the coat of arms of the Port of London Authority.

I translated his words as best I could, and received the impression that Anton was quite overcome with what was happening to him during his first morning in England – and so were we!

＊　　　＊　　　＊　　　＊　　　＊　　　＊

A few days later Anica and Anton were sitting close together on a bench beside the fish-pond at *Butterfields*, while their children hovered in the background and Damir demanded another ride round the garden in the big wheelbarrow. Anton looked a different man from the anxious and exhausted traveller who had landed on our doorstep the previous week. And the fleeting glimpses of contentment, love and happiness which touched Anica's face made our ordeal at London Airport melt away into the realms of fantasy.

Feeling rather guilty and neglectful of the other families, we paid a visit to Janja and Katica later that day. The interior of No. 3, Meadow Cottages was like the stage set for a classical drama. Poor Katica had red swollen eyelids and cheeks blotched with tears when she told us that her husband was on duty at the Maslenica Bridge again, and there had been some heavy shelling in that area during the past few days. It was the vital link on the Croatian Adriatic Highway, between the Zadar Peninsula and the Serb-controlled hinterland. Natali confirmed this, with a heart-rending sob from the depths of the armchair opposite the television set.

Janja, clearly, did not approve of these displays of weakness. She pursed her lips – a dramatic Balkan purse, quite different to its puerile Anglo-Saxon counterpart – and sternly announced; "My Filip, he come very soon. I speak plain words to him on telephone, and he come!"

Antonija, Anton and Anica with Dosco in the garden at Butterfields.

Chapter 12 - The Letter

A very interesting article appeared in the Saturday Times Magazine towards the end of June, under the heading of: "BOSNIAN CHILDREN IN BRITAIN – the rescue that went wrong."

Apparently a group of kind-hearted Wiltshire people had decided to give seventeen Bosnian children a six-month break from the war – but the 'refugees' were not quite what their rescuers expected.

Most of the organization, and the finding of seventeen hand-picked foster families, was done by Nick and Lorraine Solomon, a couple who had been deeply touched by the news coverage of the gruesome massacres at Srebrenica in April. Scenes of desperate mothers throwing their babies into over-crowded lorries to try and save their lives from the brutal Serb soldiers haunted many people at that period, but the Solomons were among the few who decided to DO something about it, beyond sitting in an armchair and clucking with moral outrage.

Nick had driven 65 tons of food and medical aid out to hospitals and orphanages in Croatia by October, 1992, while his wife had made a name for herself collecting supplies from local firms, and raising money by arranging darts matches and jumble sales in the little town of Westbury.

Later that autumn, a Croatian social worker whom Nick had met during one of his journeys rang to ask if there was any chance of him finding homes for twenty-four children in England, and she faxed some heart-breaking details about the things they had endured. Owing to passport problems, however, only seventeen of them eventually reached Wiltshire the following January; and it was not long before Lorraine discovered a few of the difficulties involved in running an amateur foster society.

Some of the would-be foster families were taken aback when a number of lusty teenagers sprang out of Mick Gelsthorpe's coach, which they had come to meet. They had been expecting small starving children, innocent victims of the brutal senseless civil war; and some foster-parents were hoping for orphaned infants who would be available for adoption. Most of these youngsters had at least one parent still living and, furthermore, they were not Bosnians – but Croatians who were turned out of their homes a year earlier during the siege of Vukovar, and had been living since then in teeming refugee camps on the Istrian coast.

The Solomons were told by a neighbour that they had been conned, and some of the foster families backed out when they discovered there were no babies for adoption, while others, clearly, had little sympathy for their charges. In one home a boy accidentally set fire to his bed.

"He seemed to spend all his time in his bedroom under punishment, so that was a bad choice of foster-parent," Lorraine admitted.

All the children had been lectured back at home that they must be polite and grateful to their English hosts.

"How do you like it here?" one boy was asked by a local resident.

"Perfect," he replied. "Everything is perfect."

"So you would like to stay here?"

"No, I would not. I want to go home."

Later he revealed that he found the food disgusting, and did not want to be away from the place where he was born for too long.

Another fifteen-year-old boy who spoke excellent English was exasperated by what he regarded as a setback to his education. "The work is easy," he said. "I did it two years ago. Our lessons at home are harder." He was worried that he was falling behind with his studies.

The Solomons themselves were recently presented with a £954 phone bill, run up by a desperately homesick girl who phoned her family back in Croatia three or four times a day. Another girl, placed with an elderly couple, was nearly expelled from school for fighting when other children called her names. She would give people she liked a good hug and the local girls resented it and started calling her Marella the Gorilla.

Ros Finlay of the British Refugee Council, who is also a part-time psychotherapist, argues that quite a lot of the psychology of these people who offer to foster refugee children is to do with power. "There's a certain something about beating the system: the end justifies the means as long as the end is good and glorious. The end stops with rescuing the children from the jaws of hell. Some of these people feel that they deserve the children more than their natural parents. It's like the judgement of Solomon; who should have these youngsters? The families to whom they belong or the ones who can protect them from danger?"

The seventeen Wiltshire children, in the meantime, have been promised that they can return to Croatia this month. But there is no money left for the journey, which will cost £4,500. The children are now toiling through sponsored bike rides and walks to raise the cash to go home.

Lorraine declares that she doesn't think she'd do it again because of the situation in which they landed themselves. "But someone has to do something," she pleads.

Thinking about it afterwards, we realized that the Wiltshire children came from refugee camps in the same area as our own families, and some of them originated from the same part of Croatia. We remembered Mick mentioning them soon after he brought them to England in January, and I felt very sad that the whole enterprise had been such a dismal failure.

I wrote to the Editor of the Saturday Times Magazine that week, and he printed my letter the following month.

10th July 1993

"Dear Sir,

BOSNIAN CHILDREN

I read 'Bosnian Children in Britain: the rescue that went wrong' with great interest, as my husband and I have been looking after fourteen refugees (four mothers and ten children) from the former Jugoslavia since last November. They were brought to England in similar circumstances to the ones described in your article.

They also, much to our initial surprise, turned out to be Croatians and not Bosnians, who lost their homes and all their possessions in 1991 during the siege of Vukovar and the occupation of Krajina by the Serbs.

We have been able to house the four families in a large flat and a cottage very close to where we live, and the children attend two excellent Roman Catholic schools in Mansfield, ten miles away.

Apart from the size of our first phone bill and the comments on our educational standards by some of the teenage girls, there are very few similarities between this group and the children who were taken to Wiltshire. Our families were greeted with great kindness by many of their English neighbours in this remote district when they first arrived, and our vicar mentioned their plight to the Directors of Center Parcs, who generously gave them fourteen bicycles.

The families have been quite an eye-opener to all of us with their old-fashioned values and standards of behaviour, their beautiful manners, the amazing discipline the mothers exert over their children, and the happy relationships many of the children have formed with their classmates and some of their elderly neighbours at home.

Although our group are well past the original six months for which we were expecting them to stay, they all seem to be settling down here very happily. Their long-term future is still undecided, but all I can say is that I hope they will stay. They are a joy to have as friends and neighbours, and perhaps they may teach us a few lessons many of us, sadly, have long since forgotten.

Yours sincerely,
ROZELLE RAYNES
(Perlethorpe, Nottinghamshire)"

Two or three weeks passed before THE LETTER came. It had no address to which one could reply, no date and no signature at the end. It read as follows:

"Yes, well, you want them to stay (14 'refugees') you pick up the bloody bill.

It's not surprising this country is going bankrupt with all these scroungers we have to keep.

Apparently this country cannot afford to pay its old age pensioners a decent pension, yet at the same time 'refugees' live a life of Riley with every benefit in the book thrown at them.

SOD OFF and take your 'refugees' with you."

"Well, what d'you think of that?" I asked Cynthia next day, after she had read the letter.

"There are plenty of turds about in this world," she observed; "but only the real scum are too scared to put their names and addresses to that sort of letter. I bet they'd never stand up and say things like that to your face."

*   *   *   *   *   *

After making a public declaration that the inhabitants of Nottinghamshire were more sympathetic and altogether nicer people than those of Wiltshire, we had a nasty shock the following week when something very unpleasant occurred at No 3, Meadow Cottages.

It was about eleven o'clock at night, and Janja and Katica and their children had just gone upstairs to bed, when they heard someone outside the front door kicking it with heavy boots and hammering on it with iron fists. They were all petrified. In a fraction of a second the two mothers were transported back to a similar situation nearly two years ago, when the Serb thugs had come to their homes in the middle of the night and set fire to everything in sight, while all around them men were being tortured, women raped and small children kicked aside and murdered.

Even Janja was much too upset to open the curtain an inch or two and look out of the upper window to see who was there. The idea of going downstairs to phone Malcolm seemed far too dangerous, as they were expecting the house to be broken into at any minute.

The battering on the door stopped – as suddenly as it had started. There was, they said, no padding of retreating footsteps nor the engine of a car revving up; nothing but small country sounds like the hooting of an owl and some sheep bleating in the field beyond the Post Office. No one was able to sleep in the cottage that night, and when Cynthia phoned to tell us what had happened next day we soon realized that it was going to be a difficult task to reassure Janja and Katica about the safety of living there.

Various people had their own theories on how to deal with this nightmare, should it recur. I wanted to attach a bucketful of water to a hook, high up under the porch, and if the villain came again I would pull on a piece of string leading in through the bedroom window, which would cause the contents of the bucket to empty itself over the head(s) of anyone beneath it. But Janja said "No, I would never have the courage to approach the window and pull on the string. And if I did, suppose this inflamed the person outside to even worse excesses?"

Stan Hodgkinson, the Head Keeper, said he would patrol the road past Meadow Cottages several times each night, but he MUST have some sort of description of the person he was looking for, should it happen again. Rowan and Janet, who can see No 3 across the fields from their upper windows, promised to swoop down on the house immediately, if someone could only pick up the phone and dial their number. But Malcolm produced the best idea of all by adding an extension to the telephone line, thus making it long enough to use the instrument from upstairs in the first bedroom.

The nightmare did recur – in fact, once a week for the next month, but never on the same night each week. Janja grabbed the phone on the second occasion and dialled Cynthia's number; and she and Malcolm leapt out of bed and reached the house in two or three minutes. But it was all over by then, and there was no trace of a strange car, nor a group of drunken louts, nor anyone suspicious lurking round the back. For some unknown reason, it never occurred while we were at home. I found this strangely disturbing as I would have loved to come face to face with the perpetrator of such a mean and cowardly act.

I believe Malcolm phoned Rowan on the third occasion, and he shone a very powerful torch on the cottage and thought that he saw someone scurry behind the bushes – but he was too far away to be sure. Some of the other occupants of Meadow Cottages admitted hearing unusual noises on several occasions late at night; but no one volunteered to rush outside and leap on the culprit next time it happened.

So poor Katica and Janja and the four children lived in a state of deep anxiety for several weeks – until the glorious evening when Filip and Milan drove into Perlethorpe village.

Chapter 13 - Decisions

"Can you go Heathrow Saturday?" An excited voice called over the garden wall. "My Milan come with Janja's Filip, by *Slovenski* Airline from Ljubljana at 1600 hours."

We were due to leave Butterfields that Saturday anyway, and travel to Dover the following morning after a night in London.

"*Supair!*" I called back, feeling it was just the reverse as we had only three or four days in which to make some complicated arrangements for meeting the two husbands and getting them back to Thoresby afterwards. But it was our idea in the first place, Dick pointed out, so we had to see it through however inconvenient it might be.

Big John came to our rescue in the end. He volunteered to drive down to Heathrow with Dragana and Natali and meet us there just before the plane was due to land; then bring the two men and their daughters back to Perlethorpe as soon as we had extricated them from Immigration. Everyone was delighted with this plan and all the children wanted to go with Big John, but there was no more room in his small car with the fathers and their luggage to fit in on the return journey.

We made all the arrangements with John over the telephone, and it was not until some while afterwards that we heard about his operation for a stomach ulcer which had taken place that week, and how he had discharged himself from hospital against the advice of his doctor and the nurses so that he would not let us down.

We all arrived at Terminal 2 in good time and met near the information desk in the Arrivals Hall. John was wearing his thick brown sweater and woolly cap to match, with an impressive emblem stitched on the front of it. The two girls were very excited, but Dragana looked strong and composed while Natali kept sinking on to a bench and saying that she felt faint and her legs were about to collapse beneath her!

I took photographs of John and the girls outside the toy shop, posed beside a six foot tall Teddy Bear dressed in a red and gold uniform with a black velour hat on his head; then we all had coffee and sandwiches in the cafeteria, and John told us about his plans for returning to Croatia in the autumn.

The plane from Ljubljana landed on time, and we stood around for half an hour or so waiting for the passengers to come through the exit gate. Poor Natali suddenly sank down on to a luggage trolley, then implored me to take her to 'Toilets' as she felt sick. We hurried across the hall and the woman in charge of the Ladies' Room exclaimed "Not you again!" with a big grin. We had got to know each other quite well during Anton's drama with Immigration the previous week.

"Natali! Hurry up, or we might miss your father when he comes through the gate," I battered on the door of her cubicle.

She came out clutching her best mauve T-shirt, with a dead-white face and eyes filled with anguish. Dragana was waiting just outside the Ladies, and she grabbed Natali by the arm and gave her what I suspect was a stiff talking to, because she soon pulled herself together when the two men came through the exit. They had enormous smiles stretched across their faces and heavy holdalls clutched in their right hands.

Dragana's father, Filip, was a tall man wearing a grey suit and white shirt, and when he had stopped hugging his daughter and smiling I noticed that he looked bewildered, rather ill and extremely tired. We shook hands with him and said "*Dobro došli!* (Welcome!)" – and introduced him to Big John.

Then we turned round to greet Milan. About the same height as Natali, he wore an eye-catching shirt decorated with giant sunflowers and tropical reptiles against a green background, and his round sunburnt face, broad shoulders and rounded shape gave a first impression of strength and determination, coupled with a happy and optimistic nature.

Natali had tears of joy pouring down her cheeks, and as soon as the introductions were over Milan searched in his wallet for a photograph of a small puppy which he passed round for everyone to inspect.

"That is my little dog," he announced with great pride. "He lives with me in my tent."

Milan had only two and a half weeks' leave from his regiment which was having a hard time defending the Maslenica Bridge and the Zadar Peninsula; but Filip, who was still living in a refugee camp near Rijeka, hoped to remain in England for the full four weeks of his visitor's permit.

The two men had very little trouble passing through Immigration on this occasion – perhaps Dick's angry words had helped – and John was anxious to set off home as it was already seven o'clock in the evening. We walked to the car-park together and introduced Milan to our dog, Dosco, before they drove away on their long journey to Nottinghamshire.

Poor John, who must have felt very weak and ill by then, was left with the two fathers who could speak no English and eyed him with a certain amount of suspicion, and their happy daughters who, one imagines, chattered away in Croatian all the way back from Heathrow to Perlethorpe.

*   *   *   *   *   *

Anton and Milan had already returned to Croatia by the time we were able to visit Butterfields again. But Filip was still at No 3, Meadow Cottages – quite a different Filip to the one we had met so briefly at London Airport.

He looked fit and rested, and was smiling happily when we called at Janja's home to invite everyone round for tea. It was a strange party with just one family group intact, while Katica and Anica had red-rimmed eyes and Marica remained curiously aloof – perhaps pinning her hopes on Zvonko's visit at Christmastime.

Watching Janja and Filip standing near the pond gazing at the gold-fish swimming to and fro, I wondered how they could bear to be parted again in such a very short while – and what the future held in store for them. Dragana, as if she could read my thoughts, said in a serious manner; "I think I should go back to Croatia to catch up with my studies. All the time we stay in England I am two years behind what we learn in my country, so how would I ever pass my big exams?"

"I don't know," I admitted; "but do you really want to go back to all living together in one room again, until there is some hope of getting a proper home together?"

Janja and Filip in the garden at Butterfields.

Natali looked as if she might burst into tears at the thought of her best friend going away and leaving her, so I hastily changed the subject and asked Antonija if she would like to play the piano.

We called at Meadow Cottages to say goodbye to Filip later that week. The family were all together in the sitting-room watching television, and Filip got up from his deep armchair – how tall he seemed under that low ceiling – and made a rather formal speech in Croatian. I wondered what was on his mind and Dick, I noticed, was also looking slightly apprehensive; but after a few "*Polako molims* (Slowly pleases)!" from me, I was able to translate the gist of his remarks into English.

"I wish to thank you from the depths of my heart for the way in which you have looked after my family," he said. "I came here with no knowledge of what to expect, and I have found them well and happy, living in a nice house, and feeling safe and contented under your protection. My family and I will never forget you and we hope, one day soon, to offer you hospitality in our home in Croatia."

He bowed and then we said goodbye – fourteen kisses each from Meadow Cottages at that period.

"Let's hope he hasn't heard about the thug kicking the door late at night!" I murmured to Dick as we drove away.

* * * * * *

August was the month of heart-rending decision-making. Anica would creep up on us as soon as we approached the Stables' courtyard, and entice us through a doorway into some dark room like the coal store beneath their flat.

"I wish to speak to you in private," she would whisper; "without all the children and the whole world listening." Her fingers fluttered in the air to indicate countless pairs of inquisitive ears twitching to hear our conversation.

"You must tell me what to decide – what is best for us to do? Anton writes that we should return to Croatia and he will find us a room in one of the refugee hotels again, and come to see us whenever he has leave. Antonija says she will stay behind in England if we try to leave – she loves this country, and there is that boy in the village who makes sheep's eyes at her every day! Marjan, on the other hand, says he refuses to learn another word of English in school if we stay; he feels he is deserting his homeland and he wishes to join the police force as soon as he is old enough."

"How about little Josip?" Dick asked.

"He is like a see-saw," Anica replied, her elbows pushed out and rocking to and fro. "He has many friends at school, the Headmaster says he is a good boy, and he listens to both sides but does not wish to upset the plum-cart, you understand?"

"Apple-cart!" I laughed; but there was little enough to laugh at that day.

Anica was being torn into shreds by her family and wanted us to make up her mind for her – to say something decisive. But that was the one thing we could not do.

"Only you can decide what is best for you and your family," I told her. "We hope that you will stay for ever and ever and we shall miss you bitterly if you leave. But if you decide to go, you must realize that you will not be able to change your mind and return here if life is too hard in Croatia. You would only get permits to come for a short holiday, and that's all."

Marica and her family remained calm and cheerful, as if these desperate decisions did not in any way effect them. Marijana had received a ring from Robert which she showed me with great pride. Her computer course at college was going well, and she was sometimes able to earn a few pounds working in the restaurant attached to the Pierrepont Gallery, especially during busy summer weekends.

Ivana now had a special friend, Victoria, who lived in Perlethorpe and went to school on the same bus with her each morning. They had a wonderful time cycling around the park together and playing games in the village youth club, and Amelia and Bill or Eileen and Ted were always

Damir and Ivana with Dick's Lagonda in the Stables' courtyard.

there in the background, happy to entertain any of Marica's or Anica's children, or to drive the mothers into Worksop to do their shopping.

Eric, the Security guard at Thoresby House, lent the children four tennis-rackets and some balls, and a few of them played every day on the village tennis-courts which made the summer holidays fly by at an alarming speed. We were cycling across the old stone bridge that spans the River Meden one day, when Dick noticed some freshly engraved letters on the parapet. We stopped and brushed the moss aside, and there was I V A N A in big bold lettering, close to some other initials of children from the village.

"I think that's rather nice," I said. "It will be a record of her growing up here in years to come."

Unfortunately neither Dick nor Rowan agreed with me, and a certain coolness ensued between them and the young culprits until a suitable lecture had been delivered on the subject of carving one's name for posterity!

Little Damir was also very happy in England. He had many friends at school and he was busy teaching Croatian to Steve the Potter, whose workshop overlooked the far side of the Stables' courtyard. He called on Amelia regularly to play with Judy, drink Coca Cola and eat delicious bars of chocolate; and he often went cycling with the older boys or played football when Big John came over to organize their games. Everyone loved Damir and, being the youngest of the refugees, he was, perhaps, a little spoilt. But Marica remained a strict mother, even though her eyes would melt with pride when she regarded her small son.

After Filip returned to Croatia the atmosphere at No 3, Meadow Cottages became increasingly fraught. Katica was deeply engrossed with filling in some complicated forms to send to Australia House in London. Milan, who had a friend living near Sydney, was anxious to emigrate to Australia with his family and he had left the application forms for Katica to deal with. But she did not really want to go there because she had a frail old mother living near the Serb/Croat border in Krajina, and a married sister near Karlobag, and she thought she might never see them again if she went to live so far away. She was quite relieved, I believe, when Meggi found out that her family were unlikely to be accepted because they could not speak much English, had no home offered to them in Australia, nor did Milan have a job waiting for him there – the three main criteria required of new immigrants in 1993.

Janja, unlike her normal self, was torn with indecision and wanted our advice on whether to stay or go. She could visualize quite clearly the life to which they would be returning; but there was Filip to think of, living in the refugee camp all by himself; and Dragana, constantly worrying about her education and how much she was missing by remaining in England. Then Filip wrote to say that he had been promised two rooms (an unheard of luxury) in a hotel at Kostrena if his family came back, and he had reserved places for the children in the best schools in the neighbourhood, but must let them know, one way or the other, very soon.

Next morning when Katica led us into the kitchen, Janja's profile reminded me of Montenegro – a landscape of harsh rocky contours, devoid of all softness. Natali sobbed piteously from the depths of the big armchair in the sitting-room and Dragan did some furious pumping to the back tyre of his bicycle, which was leaning against the shed.

Janja rose to her feet and embraced us both, then announced in a firm voice; "We go. Can you fix seats on aeroplane to Ljubljana, before end of August, please?"

                    *   *   *   *   *   *

Nottingham Radio phoned us at the beginning of August to say that they intended to make a programme on an old bus driving round Mansfield, and it was to be filled with interesting local personalities with a story to tell; so would we care to bring some of the Croatian children along to be interviewed? One child from each family, they stipulated, as there would not be time to speak to all of them, as well as us and a few other special people.

The invitation was so flatteringly worded that it sounded irresistible! We asked each mother in turn and they all said the boys were too shy and would only giggle if they knew their voices were going out 'live' on the radio; so Dragana, Natali, Ivana and Antonija became the chosen four who accompanied us to Mansfield on that hot summer's day.

The bus was a treasure of a 1939 model, and a very talkative lady who boarded it at the same time as our party declared that she was responsible for our invitation as she was a member of St Edmund's Church Council, and she had remembered the refugees with great pleasure from the reunion her vicar had arranged in the church hall, soon after the Croatians arrived last November.

The driver took his seat and the radio interviewer, a man with reddish hair and a wispy moustache and beard, tested his microphone and shouted a few instructions at the driver of a white limousine nearby. It had an extraordinary-looking ridged column sprouting from its roof and NOTTINGHAM RADIO proclaimed in red and blue lettering along its sides. It would be following directly behind us during the programme, the radio man informed us, and he would interview each of us in turn, for three minutes exactly, as soon as we were under way and travelling slowly across Mansfield.

Natali and Ivana cleared their throats nervously and whispered to me; "What will he ask us?"

Antonija combed her long gold tresses and Dragana looked rather fierce and determined. Dick was in the middle of an interesting discussion about old engines with the bus driver when the radio man said sharply; "Everyone keep quiet now, till I speak to you. We're off."

The driver engaged the gear lever and the bus leapt forward into the busy afternoon traffic of Central Mansfield. I looked over one shoulder and saw the white car turning left into the same street, but it was unable to swerve round the flank of a rather pushy van which was now following directly behind us.

"Bugger!" said the radio man – I wondered if his microphone was switched on – "that's torn it. Have to hold our fire till we reach the top of that hill."

The children were not at all dismayed by the change in the programme, and began to giggle and tell me funny things in Croatian across the gangway. By the time we reached the top of the hill the white car was no longer in sight; and a Spanish lorry, a Range Rover and a car towing a caravan had inserted themselves behind the pushy van.

"Terribly sorry, folks, but the white car's gone missing, so we'll have to wait now till we both reach the car-park in Mansfield Woodhouse. We should be on the air in two minutes' time, but I expect they'll play some old records instead." The man looked distraught and glared at our driver, then at Dick, as if he needed someone to blame for this change of plan.

"I dare say the old records will give just as much pleasure," Dick ventured; but neither the radio man nor the lady from St Edmund's allowed a glimmer of a smile to soften their angry features.

It all turned out well in the end. The white car caught up with us just as we reached the car-park, its radio aerial, which had now reached a height of twenty feet, swaying dizzily above the tree-tops as it swung round a corner into its parking space. Firmly anchored close together in the car-park, our man sprang into action and barked an order for total silence inside the bus. The questions poured out of his mouth like continuous grape-shot, and I could see Ivana gulping with fear as Ginger-head moved down the bus. All the usual old posers came out, one after another.

"How do you like living in England? Do you miss your own country? Have you made many friends at school? What will you do in the holidays?"

I cannot remember who answered which questions, but the important part was the listeners at home. All kinds of unexpected people had tuned in to Radio Nottingham that afternoon to hear The Travelling Roadshow; and no one revealed that it was not actually travelling when it came on the air. Dragana, Natali, Ivana and Antonija were treated as little heroines back in Perlethorpe that evening; and Damir, who had been forced to sit through the programme wedged between his mother and Amelia, gave his opinion that it was a load of shit!

*   *   *   *   *   *

Stan Hodgkinson's son, Granville, drove Janja and her children to London Airport on August 25th. We met them in the Departures Lounge and had a meal together at the cafeteria. After they had checked their big luggage in at the Slovenian Airlines' desk we noticed that they still had the biggest trolley full of hand luggage we had ever seen in our lives before.

"They'll never let you on to the plane with all those bags and holdalls," Dick predicted, but Janja smiled broadly and said *"Nije problema!"*

Dragan had moist eyes all through lunch, which suddenly overflowed when he opened his parting present from us – a little penknife with a big steamship engraved on the casing. Janja looked calm and resolute – she had made up her mind and that was that. And Dragana, I think, was somewhere half way between. She had shed bitter tears leaving Natali back at Thoresby, but now she would face the future with her head held high and a smile on her lips.

The loudspeaker announced the boarding of Flight 110 to Ljubljana, and suddenly the Franjković family were hung about with holdalls and heavy parcels, like pack-horses setting off into the wilds. There was just time for our last twelve kisses – six for Dick and six for me – before they were shunted towards Passport Control and Janja held out her passport with a tense expression on her face. I found myself trying to avoid Granville's eye while I snuffled into a large white handkerchief.

*   *   *   *   *   *

A few days later we received a postcard from Dragana which said:
"Dear Dick and Rozelle,

We want to tell you that we arrived well. We didn't have any problems with passports. Just the man went somewhere to check something, but everything was fine.

We arrived in Ljubljana at 7 p.m., and at 10 p.m. we went to Rijeka. This two days here is raining and windy.

This is all for now and we hope we'll hear you soon. Goodbye!

Janja, Filip, Dragan, Dragana.
xxxxxxxxxxxxxxxxxxxxxxxxxxx"

*   *   *   *   *   *

The Annual Sprint took place at Thoresby early in September – a meeting of small fast cars, as noisy as hungry lions when they roared round heavily-sandbagged corners within a stone's throw of the old house. It was a sight to delight the hearts of all the male children – between eight years old and eighty – for miles around, and we soon discovered Marjan, Josip and Damir sitting on the railings with Robert and Lee, while Ivan and a friend of his from Perlethorpe examined some of the cars at close quarters.

Anica had finally decided to return to Croatia with her family at the end of the month, so this was the last special event at Thoresby for the children to enjoy; but Antonija, who was washing up dishes with Natali in the restaurant, vowed that she would run away and hide when the day of their departure came, so that she could stay in England for ever and ever.

I watched Marjan watching the cars, and noted his secret smile. "He's happy at last," I whispered to Dick; "he's going home to fight for his country."

The autumn term started that week, so we invited the three mothers to come with us to Lincoln one day while the children were away at school. I warned them that the weather forecast was bad, so Marica and Katica wore their thick woollen trousers and anoraks with the Turkish-style scarves wound around their heads. But Anica put on her best black coat over her emerald-green dress, and some intensely smart high-heeled shoes – after all, it's not every day you get invited to lunch in Lincoln, she argued.

We drove across the flat green landscape, through swirling mist and driving rain. The donkey sanctuary appeared briefly on our left side, then there was nothing but green and grey flatlands and big raindrops on the windows till we turned sharp right. And, suddenly, through a break in the clouds, we could see Lincoln Cathedral floating in the sky – like some enchanted building that would soon drift away on the wings of a bird.

A chorus of "*Krasnos! Divnos!*" and similar exclamations of delight reverberated round the interior of the car. That was, perhaps, the best moment of the day because it rained and rained all afternoon, and when we climbed up the steep cobble-stoned alleys to visit the Cathedral, a torrent of water rushed down towards us from above. Poor Anica, in her best clothes, was hopping from puddle to puddle with her coat and dress held high to protect them from the deluge. The others laughed without mercy because they had brought their wellingtons. But the moment we left the sodden streets and stepped inside that glorious building, Anica was the only one amongst us women who looked sublime in her surroundings!

We had lunch beside a log fire in a cosy pub, then wandered around the shops as the rain had eased a little. The mothers bought a few small gifts for their children, but nothing for themselves. I did, however, notice them gaze with longing at the windows of a shop filled with French perfumes.

*   *   *   *   *   *

Exchanging presents shortly before take-off had become a regular feature of our expeditions to say goodbye to our Croatian friends at London Airport. It was Anica's turn on September 28th, and I remember feeling very sad as we drove to Heathrow that morning. Each family was special in its own particular way, and it felt like losing a precious jewel when they left – something that could never be replaced.

We arrived there early on that bleak autumn day, and so did Anica and her family. She had very little luggage to worry about, compared with Janja. Antonija seemed to have shrunk into her jacket with misery, while Marjan was very much the man-in-charge of their travelling arrangements, seeing after the tickets, the weighing of the baggage, the loading time – everything required to get them safely back to Zagreb where Anton had promised to meet them.

I had a small bottle of *Diorissimo* to give to Anica, and she gave us a beautiful hand-embroidered tablecloth, a work of art created with her own special stitching which was quite different to the crochet-work done by the other mothers. But sometimes the most unexpected gifts can cause a sudden blaze of joy – like the one Josip produced that morning.

He fished in his trouser pocket and drew out a small parcel wrapped in grubby white paper and, offering it to me, he said; "I hope you like this! I made for you in school."

I unwrapped it very carefully and inside I found a terracotta sun with a face in the middle of it – big round eyes, tiny nostrils and a happy upturned mouth; a face to make you smile on a rainy day.

"Oh, isn't that *KRASNO!*" I exclaimed. "We'll find a very important place for it at home, and we shall remember you every time we look at it."

Lunch was a sticky meal – everyone making polite conversation for the sake of making it, and Antonija quite unable to swallow a morsel; only to gaze at the pretty gold chain Lee had given her as a parting present. Marjan's present from us was a chess-set, and as soon as the plates were cleared away he suggested us having a game. That was a splendid idea from my point of view, as it kept us busy with our heads down till loading time. We had a tough battle with no weak opponent for whom one should feel sorry, and Marjan won just as the loudspeaker started to bray "Will all passengers for Zagreb please ..."

There were no delays at Passport Control, and a few minutes later we watched the unimpressive little plane take off from below the cafeteria windows and rise swiftly into the clouds away to the south-east of London Airport.

Anica phoned us from Zagreb that evening.

"*Sve je bilo u redu,* (Everything was O.K.,)" she said. Anton was standing beside her and tomorrow they would take the bus to Lovran, near Rijeka, where he had secured two rooms for his family in the Villa Atlanta.

They were now going to work towards one big objective, she told us; to find an old ruined house they could afford, and build a family home for themselves again, so that we could be their first and dearest guests!

Chapter 14 - The Last Husband

The month of October was quiet and grey. Marica and her family moved into the small sitting-room soon after the Hržić family left; they found it cosier and easier to heat, and they would often go out with Amelia to collect kindling wood from beneath the trees surrounding the old stables.

Marijana and Ivana were able to move into their own bedrooms at last – a source of constant delight to both of them.

"Come and see my room!' Marijana proudly invited me, next time we returned to Thoresby. "I have done much work to make it nice place."

I hardly recognized it as one of the five bedrooms we had so painstakingly painted, carpeted and furnished last October. It was no longer a cramped little room in which three people and all their belongings were expected to exist; a miraculous transformation had taken place. The wall-space between Mother's watercolours of her foreign travels was adorned with pictures of film-stars, pop-singers, old friends of Marijana's from her home town and new friends from college; also there was a photograph of her father and several good ones of Robert. Special greeting cards and paper flowers decorated the mirror, while the largest Teddy Bear occupied a position of importance on a chair beside the dressing-table, and a variety of smaller bears perched on the bed with their backs against the pillow.

One big surprise was a small table acting as a desk with a typewriter sitting purposefully in the middle of it. A row of books were propped on the windowsill: an English/Croatian Dictionary, Colloquial Serbo/Croat, First Steps to using a Computer, etc. And I noticed a number of cassettes beside a small cassette-player on the dressing-table.

The room had become an extension of Marijana, an expression of her life – past, present and future. And in order to save electricity – Marica and her family were always trying to prevent us spending more money on them – there was a log fire burning merrily in the small Victorian fireplace. The whole picture made me realize how important and precious a room of her own must seem to a girl who has been forced to live in horrifyingly crowded conditions for several years.

"How long did it take you to make such a lovely room?" I asked her.

"One day, maybe two," she laughed. "I had all the thoughts in my head before the others went away, so there was really no *problema*. And my teacher at college lent me the typewriter for my studies."

Ivana was also happily engaged during those grey autumn days. She and her friend, Victoria, went to a Hallowe'en Night party dressed as witches, and they dropped in at Amelia's house to show her and Bill how they looked before the party started – also to borrow some candles and broomsticks. Whenever the two girls went out together, Victoria's mother or father would keep a close eye on their whereabouts to make sure that they came to no harm.

*   *   *   *   *   *

Life at 3, Meadow Cottages was, by contrast, rather quiet and sad during the month of October. I think Katica missed Janja's company, and found the house and garden quite hard work on her own. She worried a great deal about her mother and Milan in Croatia, and Natali was inconsolable for the first few weeks after Dragana's departure. Ivan, luckily, had some friends of his own in the village; but, even so, he must have found the atmosphere at home quite depressing.

We received a letter from Janja and Dragana early in October which told us something of their life in Kostrena:

"Dear Dick and Rozelle,

We would like to thank you for your letter and card. We are alright, we all missing England. The school is began on Monday (last). I'm going to school which is called Turistic School, it seems very hard, but I must do it for myself and for my parents.

The weather is not something special, but isn't so bad. If you'll be in touch with Cynthia can you ask her did she get our postcard. In my school I have to learn croatian, english, german and italian language, and I travel every morning to school and back. To go to school I lose nearly one hour. Ones more I would like to thank you for everything. And I hope we'll keep in touch.

We send you lots of kisses and good wishes.

Love,

Dragan, Dragana, Janja and Filip

My mother will write something on croatian."

Janja's letter told us that they had had a good journey back to Croatia without a single problem – only Janja, I thought, could have entered the cabin of an aeroplane with that vast mound of luggage and got away with it. Then she thanked us for all our help and the farewell presents which had brought so much joy to herself and Filip. And, finally, she sent warm greetings and many kisses to me and *Gospodinu Diku* (Dick), *Sintiji* (Cynthia), *Molkomu* (Malcolm) and *Đanet* (Janet) and all their other friends at Thoresby. And she demanded that we should write again SOON.

*   *   *   *   *   *

Anica's first letter came a few days later – two closely written pages in Croatian which gave us a clear picture of her life in Lovran.

The journey to Zagreb had been without problems. Anton had met them at the airport and brought them to his sister's house, then they travelled in a bus to the coast the next day. It was raining hard when they arrived there. Immediately they had settled down in their two rooms at the Villa Atlanta, but Anton had to return to his compulsory army duties near Zagreb.

Marjan and Josip started school the next day but she was having endless problems with Antonija, to find a school to which she would consent to go. They had enough food to eat, the boys had plenty of friends and she hoped that everything would get better in time. Her brother was preparing to emigrate to Australia, and she felt very unhappy because he was going so far away.

Yesterday she had paid a visit to Janja and Filip at Kostrena, and all their family were well. She was expecting her Mama to visit her very soon. Her youngest sister was working in Germany and could not return to Croatia except, perhaps, she might come back for Christmas as they had not seen each other for a long time. Her other sister who lived in Slovenia had three young children and could not get away – except, perhaps, for a weekend.

She spent most of her free time doing 'hand-work' (embroidery, etc.), and sometimes she went fishing with Josip when he was not at school. There was no telephone at the Villa Atlanta, so they had to go to the Post Office if they needed to make a call. The children often spoke about us and Antonija said she MUST come to England again, even it it was only for a holiday. Her mother told her she might be able to go if she worked really hard at school. She said that she wished she had remained in England when her family returned to Croatia; but, of course, that would not have been possible.

Then Anica asked numerous questions about us and Dosco: were we working hard? How was life in London? Did we still go to the boat? How was Dosco after his training school? This was followed by a great many thanks, and vows that she and her family would never forget us.

The situation was still very tense in Croatia, she continued, and the owners of the Villa Atlanta were hinting at getting rid of all the refugees and selling the hotel to a foreign company next spring. If that happened, God alone knew where they would go? But all five of them wished to send us their warmest greetings and love and many kisses, and she prayed that God would guard us and grant both of us long lives filled with happiness.

And, finally, she commanded us to write very soon!

*   *   *   *   *   *

A big surprise awaited us on our return from London on November 13th. Approaching Meadow Cottages to greet Katica and her family after our absence, I sensed an aura of breathless suspense – like a coiled spring – waiting for us behind the door. Katica ran out and kissed us on both cheeks, her blue eyes sparkling with excitement; then Natali came out and kissed us on both cheeks, closely followed by Ivan who did the same: but that was the vital moment when we could see beyond Ivan's head into the kitchen – and there sat Milan, larger than life!

"*Dobro došli!* (Welcome!)" Dick exclaimed, advancing towards the man with an outstretched hand. "We are very glad that you could get leave again so soon."

But that was the crux of the whole situation. Milan did not have leave, but had finally decided that he could not bear to remain in the Croatian army any longer. His puppy had been run over and killed by a lorry just before he applied for a week's compassionate leave to visit his sick mother. And he flew back to England with a one way ticket. He knew that he might be shot as a deserter if he ever attempted to go back home.

During his first few weeks in England Milan seemed rather dour and moody. He had given up all alcohol – he had been, apparently, a notable drinker in the past – and spent most of the day crouched in front of the television set with thunder-cloud expressions flitting across his face when forced to meet any new people.

Looking back at those days, I can see that he must have been a very worried man. He had burned his boats in Croatia and had no idea whether the British Immigration Authorities would allow him to stay beyond the six month period allotted for a Visitor's Permit. It brought the ethics of a civil war sharply into focus for us. How would one behave in similar circumstances? If one was a conscript, and not a regular soldier, was it so wrong to escape from all the atrocities and bloodshed, possible orders to murder old people and children or one's former school-friends or workmates, and even to stand by helplessly while young girls were raped .

in front of one's eyes?

When we came to know him better we realized that Milan was a good man with a kind heart. He was also a very hard worker whose chief desire in life was to make a proper home for his family and live at peace with his neighbours.

There was one gleam of sunshine among the dark clouds that hung over him that autumn. Big John called at the cottage to say goodbye to his old friends in mid-November, before returning to his work in Croatia for another long stint; and he brought with him some eight weeks'-old puppies which were hardly as big as a man's hand.

"I'm trying to find homes for this lot before I go," John told the children. "Their mum's a grand little bitch – half French bulldog and half summat else – but we can't cope with any more in my place and I don't want them to go to bad homes, see?'

Ivan had already slipped indoors and, grabbing his father by the arm, he rushed him outside to the gate. Milan took one look at the smallest puppy on the back seat, picked him up gently with a hand the size of a cantaloupe melon and smiled at last – a huge broad smile like the one we had seen at London Airport.

"We call him Rex!" he said to John. "And you must have no worries. Here he will live like dog in the Queen's palace."

*   *   *   *   *   *

Dick and I received an official-looking letter in December from a Mr Alex Melbourne, Volunteer Recruitment Coordinator for the Pakrac Work-Camp. It ran as follows:

"To whom it may concern,

I wish to confirm that John Abbott of 56, Brown Avenue, Mansfield, participated in the Social Reconstruction Project in Pakrac, Croatia, from 17th November – 27th December, 1993. This project is jointly organized by the Anti-War Campaign Croatia and UN agencies in the area, primarily the UNOV (United Nations in Vienna) office in Pakrac. The town was devastated during the war in 1991-1992 and is currently divided by a cease-fire line, so that part of the town is under Serb control. The project works alongside local work-brigades and inhabitants, helping them rebuild the social and physical infrastructures destroyed by the war.

John, with his practical abilities and experience, was involved in various aspects of the project. In addition to a month's work helping to get a local

Ivana and her friend, Victoria, with Dosco in the farmyard at Perlethorpe.

Katica and Milan, holding Rex, in their garden at Meadow Cottages.

orphanage ready for reopening, he was also involved in the construction of a children's playground, delivering food parcels to inhabitants of remote villages in the Pakrac/Daruvar areas, driving on numerous occasions to deliver or pick up equipment, material, etc. John's hard work was of great benefit to the project, and he was able to share his knowledge and experience gained on previous visits to Croatia (Lipik) with the other volunteers. His work at the orphanage in Lipik won official praise from Colonel Cook, the initiator of the S.O.S. Children's Project.

The Project's staff, including myself, are very pleased that John intends to return to Pakrac in March for a period of six months, to continue his valuable contribution to the reconstruction project. We hope that you will offer him the sponsorship necessary to enable him to return.

With kind regards,

Alex Melbourne

"Sounds as if John has come a long way since the war started in Croatia," Dick observed, after reading the letter. "I wonder what Rowan would have to say about him now?"

"I hope he writes to tell us what's really going on out there," I mused. "I wonder how he manages to travel in and out of Croatia without any problems, as far as one can tell?"

The seed of an idea was beginning to germinate inside my brain.

*   *   *   *   *   *

Our last visit to London Airport in 1993 took place on December 11th. Marica and Damir drove to Heathrow in Granville's car, and we met them in time for lunch in the cafeteria. It was a very cheerful party – quite different to the farewell meals we had shared with Janja and Anica and their families during the summer months. Damir was dressed in his best shirt, jersey and long trousers that were normally reserved for church on Sunday – and no playing around with a football afterwards. It was his first visit to a big airport and he was intensely excited by the jumbo jets, and the sight of Concorde taking off for America. Granville and he vied with each other to pick out the largest and most spectacular-looking planes, while Marica gazed hopefully into the low grey clouds to be sure she would not miss her first sight of Zvonko for over a year.

"I think this might be the one!" Dick exclaimed, spluttering as he swallowed some hot coffee down the wrong way. "It's got the markings of the Croatian flag on its tail – see?"

We all had our noses pressed against the cafeteria windows by the time the doors were opened and the gangway wheeled into position.

"That's Papa, I can see him!" Damir shouted, as the first passenger emerged. Altogether he had seven separate sightings of men who looked exactly like Papa before we dragged him away to go to the passenger's exit in the main hall.

"This door looks like our old friend," I told the others. "I wonder how long we'll have to wait outside it today?"

I had hardly finished speaking when the first passengers from Zagreb made their appearance. Groups of two or three, the women mostly dressed in dark clothes, an impression of wartime deprivation hanging over the crowd. They kept on coming, one after another, and we began to feel exceedingly anxious, and to wonder what we should do if Zvonko had missed the plane or been kept by Immigration for questioning ... like Anton was.

"There he is," Marica suddenly sobbed into my left ear. "Mother of God, his hair has turned grey since I saw him last!"

He was one of the last to come through that fateful door, a tall handsome man with a limp who was having some difficulty in carrying his hand-luggage, searching among the sea of strange faces for his family and steering a straight course towards the final exit. He had a real Slav face – high cheek-bones and slightly triangular eyes and, not having known him a year previously, I thought his grey hair made him look very distinguished.

Dick and I turned away to put a call through to Marijana and Ivana at Thoresby, while Zvonimir (known as Zvonko for short) greeted his family. The girls were very excited when they heard that Papa had landed safely and was free to travel north immediately. A few minutes later we were back in the car-park waving goodbye to the happy Ðerđ family. Damir was sitting on one side of his father, chattering incessantly in high-pitched Croatian; Marica sat close to him on the other side with an expression of deep contentment on her face, and Granville looked resigned and rather inscrutable – he raised and lowered his eyebrows once or twice in quick succession as he took to the road.

* * * * * *

John's letter from Pakrac arrived on Christmas Eve.

20.12.93 PAKRAC

"Dear Dick and Rozelle,
Thanks for the card, it was a nice surprise for me. You say the kids are missing me, I'm missing them also very much, and I'll be very happy when I see them in February.

I have been working a lot at the orphanage in "Lipik". The children returned on 10th December, it was a great day for everyone involved, especially Goran, my friend the Director, and Colonel Mark Cook. To see the kids get off the bus, walk towards the new building crying with happiness and holding their hands together like a prayer, was very emotional – something I'll never forget. We finished work there Friday, 17th Dec, but have been told to visit whenever we want to have a game of football, table tennis, etc. with the kids, which is great news as we get on really great with them, and we are greeted with great joy when we go there.

My name is *Veliki John* (BIG JOHN) to them. I've been picked to be Santa Claus (probably because of my big belly) to the schoolchildren of Pakrac, nearly 400 in total, so at the moment I am getting very nervous. I been learnt a little Croatian, just enough to get me through <u>I hope.</u>

I have made some really good friends here, and when I leave it will be hard to say goodbye, but great to see you all at Thoresby. In 2nd week of January I'm going on a Friday to Rijeka and Opatija to see Dragana,

Antonia, etc., then return to Pakrac Sunday night, then on 1st FEB I leave Pakrac to return home to England. I will stop one night and day at my brother's near Dover, and hope to be home for 5th FEB which is my son and my grandson's birthday, same day.

So thanks for the card, it was very kind of you and I'm very grateful.

Happy Xmas and New Year,

"JOHN"

*   *   *   *   *   *

Our Christmas at Thoresby started on December 20th – a day of low grey stratus clouds and pelting rain. But the Head Forester had put a tall and beautiful Christmas tree, grown in Sherwood Forest, in our house before we arrived there, and we spent a few happy hours with Malcolm and Cynthia standing on step-ladders arguing about where to hang the little gold angels, the white reindeer, the set of coloured silk horses from Hong Kong and all the other glittery baubles and tiny lanterns which had been packed away in their cardboard box, waiting patiently for eleven and a half months for their magic moment.

The sun shone on a Christmas-card landscape next morning. The branches of the silver birch tree were transformed into a delicate white spider's web, there was a thin layer of ice on the pond and a pure white carpet of snow covering the grass.

We drove into Newark to do a mountain of shopping, then to the Stables to visit Bill and Amelia and, finally, Marica and her family. Just as the other fathers had done, Zvonko looked fitter and more relaxed after a few days in England; and he enjoyed going for a ride next morning with Dick in his Frazer Nash.

During the next few days a number of friends of Marica's and her children came to call. There was John Gradiški and his wife, who had been wonderfully kind to all our Croatians during the past year, taking them shopping in their car nearly every week; and there was Patricia, the charming girl who often brought them a present of new-laid eggs; and Monica, the Polish teacher from Ivana's school, and her best friend, Victoria, and Marijana's Robert.

Zvonko behaved as the perfect host, inviting everyone to be seated and to have a drink or some Turkish coffee with some of Marica's delicious home-made cakes. But there were times when I wondered if he might not resent all those new friends who had helped to make his family settle down so happily in England. And if anyone was foolish enough to touch on the subject of Marijana and Robert, fiery darts would appear in his eyes while he reached for another glass of *šljivovic*!

We also went to Katica's home to drink coffee soon after our arrival. The Christmas decorations in their sitting-room were quite spectacular: a big fir tree stood in the bow window adorned with musical toys as well as red, gold and green shiny baubles, Santa Claus in his sleigh and lots of glittery streamers. There was a mound of parcels stacked beneath the tree and cards suspended from a length of string stretched right across the room. "Isn't that *KRASNO!*" I exclaimed. "And it looks wonderful from outside as well – we noticed when we passed your window."

"I glad you like it," Katica beamed. "Milan and me, we go *Engleski* classes now – two times every week – so we soon speak good English!"

Rex was stretched out in front of the fire wagging his tail, the picture of a contented puppy; and Milan looked quite different from the November Milan. He had been working very hard in their large garden, digging, raking, hoeing and burning huge piles of weeds and rubbish, then pruning the small trees and preparing the ground for grass, spring flowers and vegetables; also an elegant arrangement of paving-stones leading to their door. He no longer looked dour and moody, for his whole being was straining towards the future.

"I wish to make our home a beautiful place for my family to live in," he announced with pride. "And Meggi has written to London about our work permits. As soon as they come, Katica and me we find jobs, then we can earn proper money and need not go to the Post Office each week to get money. Some people they give us bad looks when we receive that money, you understand?"

We understood very clearly, and knew how much they had suffered from certain people in the village until Steve and Sue Rose on one side and Robin Orr and his sweet girl-friend on the other had stretched out the hands of friendship across their garden fences.

Drinking coffee in Marica's flat next morning, we asked Zvonko why he did not try to stay in England with his family until the war was over.

"I have no desire to desert my country and not be able to return there, like certain people one knows," he replied haughtily. "I would only stay here if I could come and go as I pleased. But I shall have another operation done on my leg at the hospital in Zagreb very soon, and I wish to be in best position for getting home together for my family when the time is ripe." Marica and Marijana looked doubtful, and Damir said in a loud voice; " I don't want to leave England. I got friends and I likes it here."

Ivana, Marijana, Marica, Zvonko and Damir in Amelia's sitting-room at Christmastime, 1993.

*   *   *   *   *   *

Christmastime was filled with visits and parties and parcels, and a great deal of cooking; and the arrival of our old friend, Mike Uglow, at one time a doctor in the R.A.F. and now a very talented musician whose fingers could draw forth magic from the piano. He came just before our Croatian party on Christmas Eve.

Everyone arrived wearing their best clothes, looking very shy and subdued, apart from Damir who ran straight towards the tree and began to prod the parcels beneath it with inquisitive fingers.

"Come here at once, limb of Satan!" Marica ordered him. "You will receive no parcels for yourself this Christmas if you behave in that sinful way."

Zvonko regarded the boy in silence. Clearly he was entranced with this wonder-child, his only son, who had grown up so amazingly since he left Croatia thirteen months ago.

The Jerbić family sat close together on the sofa, opposite to the Đerđ family on the other sofa. Natali wore a beautiful new dress – coffee-coloured velvet with gold and silver patterns encrusted in the light brown background; and she had fixed a small bouquet of flowers in her hair. The other girls glared at her rather enviously while everyone munched their hot buttered scones and Christmas cake in total silence.

I looked at Dick who, judging by his expression, was recalling that other silent tea-party when the Croatians had just arrived at Thoresby.

"We'll make Damir into Father Christmas," he suddenly declared, fitting a red and white Christmas bonnet on to his head; "then he can read out all the names on the parcels under the tree – he might even find one with his own name on it – and deliver them to their proper owners. Afterwards we'll pull the crackers."

Damir thought this was a wonderful plan, and so did Ivana who offered to help him pass round the presents. From that moment onwards the wall of shyness fell apart. Each person received their parcel – but were given strict instructions by Marica and Katica not to open it till Christmas morning – then we stood up with all our hands crossed to pull the crackers. Soon we were wearing paper hats and puffing into balloons – Mike was by far the best puffer – and as soon as they were big enough we played balloon football; the children shrieked, Dosco barked and Milan, Zvonko, Mike and Dick threw them higher and higher so that Ivan and Damir had to jump up and down like monkeys in a cage to try and catch them.

Cynthia's daughter, Dawn, joined us about this time, quite unprepared for the boisterous games and yelps of excitement coming from the drawing-room. When everyone was tired and most of the balloons had burst, Mike played some Christmas carols on the piano; then we sat in a big circle on the floor and played Hunt the Slipper, a new experience for our guests. All too soon the mothers got to their feet and told their children and menfolk it was time to go home.

"Ada send car for us tomorrow, make sure we get to church in good time!" Marica told us; "and Santa Claus come in the night, so everyone go to bed early."

Despite our fears, it had been a very happy party after all – a Christmas Eve to remember in the months ahead.

* * * * * *

Christmas morning was pink and grey, with a hard white frost underfoot. We went to our church in Perlethorpe and prayed for peace and goodwill all over the world, but especially in Bosnia; then we sang the old familiar hymns and the spirit of Christmas hovered in the air above us. Marica and

Katica and their families were, perhaps, offering the same prayers in Ada's church in Ollerton; and Zvonko was certainly praying for the war to end very soon so that he could take his family back home.

After Christmas lunch, Mike, Dick and I opened our presents then walked to the Stables with Dosco to visit the Đerđ family. Marijana made a signal to me that she had a secret to share the moment we entered the flat, and pulled me swiftly into her room. She ran to the bedside table and opening a drawer, pulled out a small box carefully wrapped up in Christmas paper.

"You look!" she invited me, unwrapping it lovingly and handing me the box. I wondered how many times it had been opened and closed since the original unwrapping – perhaps at midnight on Christmas Eve.

"Oh, my word, what a LOVELY present!" I exclaimed, as I looked at the charming gold wrist-watch inside the box. "Who gave you that? Can I guess?"

Her eyes were like brilliant stars and suddenly she looked beautiful as she pronounced the one word, ROBERT. Lucky boy, I thought to myself; and lucky Marijana too. I just hope no one tries to put a spanner in the works.

Marica was a wonderful home-maker. The cosy sitting-room with its log fire, soft lamplight and polished furniture adorned with intricate crochet-work seemed to reflect her warm personality and happy smile as she pressed her guests to take another cup of Turkish coffee and a little glass of *šljivovic* with a slice of home-made cake.

"You eat like sparrows," she chided us. "You must try this one," producing a splendid chocolate confection decorated with almond slithers, "this is a speciality of our homeland."

After our meal we played television games with Ivana and Damir, and admired the boy's new white costume that Marica had bought him to wear for *tae-kwondo*. When the time came for us to leave, Zvonko rose to his feet and, bowing with great formality, he offered us an envelope. " You will read this later when you are at home," he instructed us.

We thanked him and Marica for their hospitality and kissed everyone goodbye. Marijana ran down the staircase to see us off and whispered to me when her father was out of earshot; "He spent many hours last night writing that letter!"

Back at *Butterfields*, I sat down at the kitchen table with my English /Croatian dictionary and translated it as best as I could:

"To Dr Dick and Rozell,
I am grateful to you from the heart for the way in which you have

received my family, and taken so much trouble to care for them and make them comfortable.

When I came to England and saw how they live, I felt happy and more than happy. When I observe how you behave with love and big open hearts towards my family, I am eternally grateful and would like to wish you a long life and much good health, and all the best wishes in life for yourselves that can be achieved.

XXXX
    Đerd Zvonimir"

"Well, isn't that a nice surprise to get on Christmas night?" I said to Dick and Mike, putting the meat in the oven to cook. "I thought his letter was going to be filled with worries and complaints about his children not wanting to go back to Croatia.

"Perhaps that's still to come!" Dick laughed. "But it must be hard for the poor man to return to the refugee camp in two weeks' time and leave his family here for, perhaps, another year or more – without much hope of making a home together in the foreseeable future."

Chapter 15 - Aid for Croatia

The Christmas and New Year celebrations were over, Zvonko had returned to Croatia and the children were back at school. The snow had all been washed away by the dismal driving rain and, one way and another, the outlook was rather bleak. It was about that time when the letters from Dalmatia and further north began to reach us.

Jakov and Matica, the former Partisans from the Island of Hvar who were our oldest friends in the former Jugoslavia, wrote that they were managing to survive thanks to their children who worked in Germany and Zagreb, but life was far from easy and they were saddened by the fact that they had not seen us for at least three years. Could we not manage to visit them in 1994?

Vera, who used to run the little *gostionica* on the Island of Brač, wrote that she and Maté were only just surviving. They earned no money as there had been no visitors on the island for two years; their tiny vineyard and vegetable plantation had yielded nothing after the terrible drought and raging fires last summer, and Jakše, their only son, had been forced to join the army and was even then facing unimaginable dangers on the Krajina/Croatian front line. Added to that, Vera herself was in constant pain and could scarcely walk because she needed a hip replacement operation; but the doctors at the hospital in Split were far too busy with the casualties being flown in daily from Bosnia to attend to any civilian problems which, in any case, would cost far too much money for them to contemplate.

Little Verica (Jakše's daughter, and their adored grandchild) was well and loved going to school (she'd had no shoes and was unable to go for many months till we sent her a pair from England). And, finally, Vera and Maté expressed deep longing to see us again, and hoped we would accept the little gift she had made us for the New Year.

Their parcel contained a very large and splendid table-cloth, worked with Vera's crochet-hooks into the most elegant design we had yet seen. It was a dream of beauty which must have taken her at least six months to make.

Anica wrote from Lovran that she and Antonija had been very ill, and she was still unable to find a proper job, apart from her *ručni rad* (handwork), which she hoped to sell to the German tourists next summer. Josip had been to Italy for Christmas – a short holiday arranged by the priest at their church – and Marjan had plenty of friends with whom to play football.

Anton came to visit them whenever possible, and he said she was getting far too thin and must try to eat more, then she would be strong enough to go out to work again. But how could she save up for their new home under those circumstances, she asked? And where would they go if the Villa Atlanta was sold to foreigners? She missed England very much and often wished she was back there, but she told herself that it was better to live a much worse life in Lovran and be near to her mother and sister and Anton, than to eat good food and feel safe, but constantly worried about her family.

A few days later Dragana wrote to ask for some recent photos of Natali, and to say that school was harder than ever and things in the shops were extremely expensive, so they needed just about everything if we were really coming to Croatia in the springtime? Janja added a short note to tell us that Filip had been back to the village where they used to live to see if there were any ruined houses to be had. But there was nothing, and the Serb shells were constantly landing on what was left. The sun was shining that morning, nevertheless, they were lucky to have two rooms at the Hotel Lucija, the food was not too bad and she prayed that we would travel safely to Kostrena in the springtime; and they awaited our arrival with joyful hearts.

*   *   *   *   *   *

After letting drop our potential plans for travelling to Croatia during a cheerful evening around Christmastime, suddenly we found that people had begun to take us seriously and there was no chance to have second thoughts!

Dick soon dismissed the idea of flying to Zagreb, as the whole point of our journey was to take as much 'aid' out there for our various friends as we could fit into a Citroen Estate. We had been told by Big John and other people that one could run into trouble crossing the Austro/Slovenian frontier where one was liable to have much of one's cargo confiscated – or be faced with demands for enormous import duties.

"Why don't we go by France and Italy instead?" I suggested. "There always used to be plenty of ferries sailing between Ancona or Bari and the Dalmatian coast."

Dick thought that sounded a good idea, so he phoned an old friend of his who had many business connections with Italy. He, in turn, faxed one of his business partners over there, who very kindly offered to assist with our hotel reservations in his country or Switzerland. He faxed back a number of delightful recommendations in Tuscany and elsewhere, but when asked about the Italian ferries running between Ancona and Split, he said there were none ... FULL STOP.

He then declared that no Italian in his right mind would dream of crossing to the coast of the former Jugoslavia! Did we have any idea of the dangers we would have to face? Had no one warned us about the refugees who were packed into the old tourist hotels in their thousands, and were all wandering about the countryside looking for trouble? They would think nothing of slitting our throats if they perceived that we had a car filled with suitcases which might contain things they could use themselves or sell on the Black Market!

I, unfortunately, had dropped a hint of our plans in my Christmas letter to an old friend in Australia. She replied briefly and tersely, by EXPRESS DELIVERY.

"You must NOT, on any account, pursue this ridiculous idea. It would be EXTREMELY foolish and dangerous to go deliberately into a war zone where such TERRIBLE atrocities are taking place every day. I shall not have a moment's peace till I hear that you have abandoned the whole project."

This sort of governessy behaviour on the part of our old friends made us more determined than ever to go. Clearly they did not wish to see the last of us which was very gratifying, but ... a few exploratory phone calls put me in touch with an obscure shipping line, the Dalmatian and Istrian Shipping Company, which was still running a ferry twice a week from Ancona to Split.

"Can you book my husband and myself and a large car on your ship the week before Easter?" I asked the man with bated breath.

"*Nije problema!*" he replied in a rich fruity voice. "You must come to Ancona on March 28th and our ship will leave for Split at 2000 hours that night. Please to send a small sum of money and we shall reserve for you a cabin for two."

If I had been in his office instead of on the end of a telephone line, I would have thrown my arms round the man's neck and hugged him! The sun came out from behind a bank of dark clouds, and we began to make long lists of all the things we planned to take with us on our journey.

Several years ago we had met a very courageous couple, Paul and Sheila Morris from Lancashire, who sailed out to Jugoslavia in their old wooden yacht, MINTHAMI, and were living aboard her in a little harbour on Hvar Island when we first came alongside them. They remained in Dalmatia after the war started, and Split became their winter base when they were not exploring the Eastern Mediterranean. The Morrises were compelled to return to England during the winter of 1993 because Sheila's mother was very ill; so we were able to have long conversations on the telephone which proved very useful indeed.

"We will make a list for you of all the things we reckon our friends in Split can't buy in the shops and need the most," Paul promised us. "Mind you, it's possible to buy most things there on the Black Market if you have enough German marks, but very few people we know can afford to do that."

Under the heading of clothing they advised thick working shirts, woollen socks and shoes for men; and dresses, skirts, blouses, shoes, wool for knitting and lengths of material for home dress-making for women. For use in the home: good soap, shampoos for washing the hair, face-cream, hand-cream, tooth-brushes, tooth-paste, shaving-cream, bath-oil, talcum powder, deodorants, washing powder for clothes. For the medicine cupboard: aspirins, paracetamol, Lemsip, Fisherman's Friends, Savlon, Anthisan, iodine, Optrex, Germaline and a number of other useful medicines which were not liable to be classed as drugs by the Customs.

Paul told us that there was a great shortage of tools for men, and our friends would be grateful if we brought out a selection of hammers, saws, sets of spanners, screw-drivers and, strangely enough, good quality padlocks which were now virtually unobtainable.

The question of food came next, and we found ourselves buying for each family giant bags of flour, yeast, rice and sugar, bottles of olive oil, a great many tins of meat and fish, as well as jams, tinned fruit and vegetables, salt, tea and coffee; and a number of last-minute supplies which we purchased in Italy like smoked ham, Dutch cheeses, spaghetti and macaroni, etc. Paul's final afterthought was a bottle of malt whisky for each of the men – especially Captain Maroević!

Then there were the children to consider: we bought two pairs of shoes, a party outfit, a red handbag, some toys and a paint-box for little Verica, and a number of presents for Janja's and Anica's children. There were two particular requests on Dragana's list: a wall-clock with a picture of Tower Bridge behind it – perhaps the day's outing to London last April had made a deeper impression on some of the children than we realized? And her second request was for a camping-stove and kettle for her mother.

The shopping took a long time and cost a great deal of money, but we had some generous contributions from friends who would have liked to accompany us on our journey. We filled fifteen suitcases and a number of smaller squashy bags by the time we had finished; and that was the limit to the amount of luggage we could squeeze inside the Citroen. Dick bought a length of heavy chain and a powerful padlock, as he thought it might be wiser to chain the suitcases together for our progression across France and Italy. We could hardly unload all our luggage, after all, at each overnight stopping-place along our route, and he thought we should sleep more soundly in the knowledge that any potential burglar would have a hell of a struggle to extract a few of our suitcases.

Three other people had been added to our list during the winter months: Katica's mother, who had made us some charming slippers for Christmas and often wrote us letters or sent messages through her daughter; Captain Maroević, who used to be the harbourmaster at Split in his younger days and was an old friend from our sailing holidays in Dalmatia; and Zvonko, living on his own at Lovran in a refugee hotel close to the one where Anica and her family lived.

*   *   *   *   *   *

Our Croatian families at Thoresby were spending a quiet winter. Ivana and Damir had been very disappointed when their mother refused to let them have one of Big John's puppies.

"We must not encourage animals to enter our home because they may cause damage to the carpets or furniture," Marica explained to them. "And it would be very ungrateful to *Gospodin* Dick and *Gospodja* Rozelle to do such a thing."

Ivana regarded her mother in silence, but Damir began to sob and to mutter "Look at Ivan, he has Rex to play with and his mother doesn't make a big fuss when Rex sits on a chair!"

Dick and I heard about these arguments, and discovered from Marica that they used to keep rabbits in the old days back in Ilok. He drove into Worksop early next morning, and returned with a handsome pair of black and white rabbits and a commodious hutch.We found an empty room in a corner of the stable-yard next to Steve the Potter's workshop, and when the children came home from school that evening there was great rejoicing.

"What are you going to call them?" I asked Ivana next day.

"Maybe Robert and Marijana!" she grinned, looking at her friend, Victoria, who was bursting her sides with suppressed giggles.

"The girl in the shop said she thought they were a pair of male rabbits," Dick told the children; whereupon Damir selected the names of his favourite Gladiators, Jet and Cobra, for HIS rabbits, as he called them.

A month later the girl in the shop was proved to be wrong, as the Đerd family woke up one morning to find six rabbits occupying the hutch!

Apart from the rabbits, Ivana and Damir had found another human friend to take them to *tae-kwondo* each week while John was abroad, and they both won trophies during the winter months – something to show with great pride to all the visitors who came to their home. A further excitement that month was provided by an old friend of ours, Dr Christopher Dowling, the Keeper of the Department of Museum Services at the Imperial War Museum, who phoned us to say that he was organizing an exhibition of drawings and paintings called "I Dream of Peace" at the museum on March 28th, and all the work on show would be by refugee children from Bosnia and Croatia. It was to draw attention to S.O.S., a Glasgow-based charity which was doing marvellous work out in Bosnia. He knew that we were interested in that part of the world, and wished to invite us to the opening party – Vanessa Redgrave, Martin Bell and various other celebrities had agreed to be there – and he wondered if we would care to bring our Croatian children along with us, as he had been unable to place his finger on any suitable ones to go with the paintings?

March 28th was the all-important date when we were hoping to embark on the Dalmatian ferry from Ancona to Split, but an invitation like that was too good to turn down when I thought of the pleasures of such an outing for our Croatians; so I did some hard bargaining with Christopher and we arranged that we would order a mini-bus (to be paid for by the museum) to bring our group to London, and he agreed to the parents as well as John Gradiški being included in the party. Janet, with her son, Jack, would travel to London by train, but meet our party outside the museum to introduce them to Christopher and the Press and television cameramen, and one child from each family would be allowed to produce something to go on show in the exhibition.

Ivana set to work immediately, and drew a scene of a village in war-time in her country which was so good that it was eventually placed as the centre-piece of the whole show in London. We were very proud of her.

The Jerbić children did not feel inspired to put pencil or paint-brush to paper, but Natali had written an essay in school for which she received top marks, and much praise from the Headmaster. I sent a copy of it to Christopher and he, also, was so impressed with it that he decided to include it among the drawings and paintings. This was what she wrote:

LIFE IN HELL

Morning ... yet another day in hell. I woke up all frozen through, hungry and completely without strength. The wind was blowing in through all the little holes as if it was also afraid of the terrifying noises of the tanks and shooting from all kinds of weapons.

Still not quite awake I thought first that I was in my own room and in my own bed, but I had made a mistake – it was not my bed ... nothing like a bed. It was only an ordinary little cellar dug deeply into the ground.

I sat on a hard rock and looked around. When I was turning around my eye caught a little boy. He was sitting in a corner all curled up into a little ball and was looking at me as if he was asking for help. His face was pale as snow as if he did not have blood in his veins, but only cold water.

One could see innocence deep in his eyes. It was such a small child, but it looked ten years older than his age, with eyes full of sadness and fear.

His lips curved into a little painful smile. Other children were crying, begging their mothers for a little piece of bread, but that sole wish nobody heard and "those people" who could fulfil it would not answer.

"Those people" will always stay in my heart and in the hearts of my contemporaries as our enemies. But why and for what reason must these little children, who do not even know what hate is, who could not harm anybody, suffer?

A few days later "those people" found us and threw us out of that wretched house. They called us names that hurt deeply in our hearts. They beat old people till they fell on to their knees and laid unconscious in the mud. Nobody would dare to help them because they would all be killed.

After a few kilometres walking they stopped us and told us to take our shoes off. Now we had to walk for two and a half hours on stones, thorns, grass and nettles wounding our feet. Only then did I notice once again that little boy I had looked at all that time before. I saw that he was walking alone; I came up to him and asked: "Where is your mum?" The little one looked up at me with his big blue eyes and that expression which broke my heart, I can still see it now. He bent his head and said: "She and my brother were killed by the people with big beards and they will also kill us!"

I noticed that he did not even wear any socks and that his little feet were covered in blood. I picked him up in my arms and slowly walked to my mother and brother. We were all hungry, thirsty, and tired out, and we desperately wanted to sit down and rest but "those people" did not let us.

After twelve hours walking we came to the camp. There we were divided – children, mothers and old people. It was horrible, One of the soldiers grabbed one of the old women and ripped her clothes, beat her up, pulled her hair out and did other awful things, just to show how he would deal with all the others if we dared to cry or make any noise. Old men were beaten with the horse whips. Those who had beards had them pulled out till they bled. After fifteen minutes of living hell, the main boss came in. My eyes filled with tears and my heart ached with sadness when I recognized him.

It was my neighbour and dearest teacher at school, the teacher I had loved as my own father, the teacher who had loved me as his own daughter. The man who had taken me to school in his car, helped me with my homework, and now turned into a cruel monster with a heart of stone. When I saw him, all my love changed into hate.

He was walking from one person to another and was saying who would be released, who killed and who would be kept imprisoned without food. When he was passing me and my brother he stopped and looked deep into my eyes. I felt a shiver going through my spine. I saw tears in his eyes – with them he was asking for forgiveness, the forgiveness that he could never get.

He got hold of my hand and said: "I am so sorry, my little one; but it is the war. I know that you despise me as much as you had loved me before. I had to do this but my fatherly love for you will never cease." My tears choked me and I couldn't even say one word.

He went away and in his way of walking I noticed that the previous proud step had now turned into one of shame and misery.

I was together with my brother put into one cold room with another twenty children. For supper we got one loaf of bread (more like stone than bread) and one litre of water.

The boy who did not have a mother fell asleep from exhaustion. Just as we were falling asleep the boss of the camp appeared in the door. He came up to me and said: "Wake your brother and the boy and quickly come with me."

I did not know if it was a dream or reality. I grabbed them both and went after him. The other children were now awake and I thought that he was going to kill us. I saw my mother in the corridor. He rushed us outside and pushed us into a jeep. I was still having an impression that it was only a dream and I could not utter a word. He had brought us to a minefield and there he left us. He had called the Croatian soldiers saying that he had a woman and three children with him. I managed to whisper only one word: "thank you". He hugged me and wished us luck.

Outside yet another bloody morning was dawning. We had to cross the minefield. We saw the lights of torches in the distance. Suddenly the little boy noticed a rabbit and started to run after it; we were not able to say anything – it was too late. He had already gone to eternal sleep. His big blue eyes drowned into the darkness and his lips still in that same smile as the first time I saw him.

There was a pool of blood around him staining the rubble that the mine had caused. Yet another young life went to eternal sleep. At least he was in the other world now, with those he loved, with his mother and brother.

There we were, safe, but how many others died, how many died of hunger? One does not even know where the graves of thousands of them are. How many have frozen to death, gone mad with fear – but the world doesn't care. Nobody cares, nobody is sorry for all those people and all those young lives. They simply sit at their tables and have their plentiful dinners. While in Bosnia and Croatia thousands of people are dying from hunger. Do they ever ask how many orphaned blind children there are, how many mothers have been left without their sons?

But they don't do anything.

People can only pray for a better tomorrow and live in hope. Their children keep asking "Why?" But nobody is going to answer, on that question.

by,
Natali Jerbić

*   *   *   *   *   *

The date of our departure was drawing near when Dick had an anxious thought: "Supposing they take us for Black Marketeers or common or garden smugglers when we arrive in Split with our fifteen suitcases," he reasoned; "wouldn't it be a good idea to try and take with us some kind of official letter saying that we are ordinary respectable people, just going to visit some old friends whom we haven't seen for a long while?"

"Yes, it certainly would," I agreed; and Rowan, who knew of Dick's worries, declared that he had a cousin out in Bosnia who was very close to General Rose*, and he could, if we liked, try to get in touch with him and ask if he could help?

We thought this sounded a splendid idea so Rowan set to work with his fax machine; but the result was very disappointing.

"Tell them not to attempt such a journey," the machine advised next day. "We have enough trouble with the official Charities who send Aid out here and require armed escorts for their vehicles, so the last thing we want is
*(then Commander of UN Forces in Bosnia.)

Natali at Thoresby - Spring 1994.

all and sundry arriving on the scene and making a nuisance of themselves."

So much for our first line of approach. Next morning we phoned the secretary of the British/South Slav Society (having been members for a good many years), but he told us that other members who had taken Aid to the former Jugoslavia – like, for instance, their President, Sir Fitzroy Maclean, – had gone as representatives of some well known Charity. He advised us to do the same or, at least, to get in touch with the Foreign Office and ask for their guidance.

The Foreign Office threw up invisible hands in horror at the other end of the line and implied that they would rather not know of our existence; but should we get into God alone knew what sort of trouble while we were out there, they were prepared to reveal the name and address of the British Consul in Split. I thanked them in my most treacly voice and extracted it from them straight way, in case they should have second thoughts in a few minutes time!

I was expecting, I cannot imagine why, a typical English name living in, perhaps, Villa Mimosa, or some similar address; so it was a complete surprise when the voice on the other end of the line spelt out a totally Slav name and address.

It had now become transparently clear that no one of any importance whose name might have impressed the Croatian Immigration Authorities wished to be associated with our venture. We were in rather low spirits that evening when we went to the Royal Cruising Club's (R.C.C.'s) monthly dinner. But they gradually rose after putting our problem to Christopher Thornhill, a famous seafarer in northern waters.

"You might try a phone call to Colin de Mowbray," he suggested. "He's the one person I know who can wave a magic wand to get some difficult bit of cargo transported to any remote part of the globe you care to mention. Take last week, for instance: our Seamanship Medal has been won by a chap who is living, at present, in South Georgia, that tiny island down in the Antarctic Ocean. Well, Colin got the navy to take it out to the Falkland Islands where the Admiral-in-Charge was persuaded to slip across to South Georgia and make a formal presentation!

"Yes, you try Colin. I'm sure he'll have some idea of how to tackle your problem."

I did try – and Colin had the jewel of a good idea.

"Why on earth don't you get in touch with Ewen Southby-Tailyour?" he asked. I believe he's an E.C. Monitor out in Split at this moment, and he'd certainly be able to tell you how to set about getting all your contraband through the local Customs!"

"Well, for one thing I hardly know him," I demurred. "It's quite a few years ago that we used to meet on the R.C.C. Committee each month."

He had done all those marvellous things during the Falklands' War, I recalled: he'd spent two years among the islands as a Royal Marine, and had charted every little harbour, anchorage and landing-place he could find. Then, when the war started, he led the Task Force into battle, flying the R.C.C. burgee from the mast of his landing-craft.

"I expect he'd love to see a couple of R.C.C. members out there," Colin broke in on my thoughts. "I'll give Patricia, his wife, a ring tomorrow and see if she has his phone number."

By the middle of March everything was fixed. We had had several invigorating talks over the phone with Ewen who managed to convey something of the atmosphere of his surroundings down the line. He made Split sound quite commonplace and yet, at the same time, like a city perched on top of a powder-magazine. He booked us a room for the night we planned to be in the city, at the Hotel Split, a huge concrete block which housed part Bosnian refugees, part E.C. Monitors and part oddments like us who were in transit to other parts of the country.

"You shouldn't have any problems with the Customs unless you're bringing in a load of Kalashnikovs," he assured us with a throaty gurgle. "And there'll be someone here to receive you when you reach the hotel, to steer you past the sentries and barricades up to my room."

Ewen had very kindly arranged for us to leave about ten of our suitcases in his bedroom while we went visiting among the nearby islands. We did not want our families in Hvar and Brač to see the car stuffed with luggage, when only a small proportion of it was for each of them. And, I suppose, at the back of our minds lingered a warning note from the Italian's earlier comments on the Bosnian refugees.

"If I'm out, my opposite number, a delightful Irishman called Fergus Marshall, will be waiting to receive you in Room 507," he told us; "and when you return to spend the night in Split after your visit to Brač, we'll get together for a meal and a chat. No need to fuss about the Customs – Fergus had a word with them yesterday and they seem to welcome the English coming through, especially anyone who looks remotely like a tourist! So I'll hope to see you at breakfast-time on Tuesday, March 29th."

*   *   *   *   *   *

The obscure little Croatian tourist office in a street behind Shaftesbury Avenue had been the last word in efficiency with all our other arrangements in their country. Two days before our departure we collected

our ferry tickets from Ancona to Split, insurance for the car, vouchers for
one night at the Hotel Kastil at Bol – they said it was the only hotel on
Brač Island that had not been requisitioned for the refugees – then three
nights at the Hotel Mina in Jelsa, Hvar Island, covering the Easter
weekend. There were more ferry tickets – another overnight voyage from
Split to Rijeka – and a further three nights in a hotel in the neighbouring
town of Opatija, close to Anica's and Janja's refugee hotels. Afterwards
we planned to drive home across Istria, Slovenia, Austria, Germany and
France.

The March days flew by in a whirl of preparations. There were parcels
to collect from Marica and Katica for their families in Croatia, and others
from Amelia and Cynthia to their friends; German marks to be concealed
in the most unlikely places, last minute thoughts about extra food-stuffs to
purchase, Dosco to leave at the kennels near Sevenoaks and some final
phone calls to our friends at Thoresby.

"Have a wonderful day in London when you go to the opening of 'I
Dream of Peace' Exhibition," I wished Katica, feeling rather envious that
we would not be there to share their glory.

"Thank you, thank you! Travel safely and a thousand kisses to you and
Gospodin Dick. Embrace my mother for me and please bring back for us a
little packet she prepares," she sobbed into the phone.

And suddenly it was March 23rd, the day of our departure.

PART 2
TO CROATIA

The western side of the Balkans

Chapter 16 - Across Europe

Ominous clouds like sleek black racing-cars came rushing towards us from Cap Gris Nez, and the weather side of the PRIDE OF DOVER was white with breaking wave-crests that mingled with the driving rain.

"Keeps the passengers nice and quiet, I can tell you!" confided our friendly steward, balancing two plates of Lancashire hot-pot on a tray on his left shoulder, with his feet clamped to the deck at an angle of 60° to the horizon. "Always like this during the equinox period," he continued; "if you're familiar with this crossing?"

"Yes, very!" I laughed, and Dick told him that I'd been a crew member of one of the cross-Channel ferries when he'd first met me.

The remainder of our voyage to France was filled with lunch and happy reminiscences of how it used to be in the days when there was only a handful of ferries crossing the Dover Straits. All too soon the twin pierheads at Calais slid past the bleary portholes and the purser's voice advised the passengers: "Please rejoin your cars now."

We drove off the ship into France, and there followed a few magic moments when I realized that all the months of planning, worrying about this and that, shopping and packing our battalion of suitcases was past. We had left England at last and this time next week, with a little luck, we might be back in our beloved Dalmatia.

The rain beat down upon the roof of the car like a serenade of tom-toms, the windscreen wipers whirred frantically to and fro and the gale roared between the tall concrete buildings as Dick drove gingerly through the empty streets.

"Hardly call this ideal motoring weather," he muttered as we drew up outside a wine shop.

After selecting a few special bottles of Benedictine, champagne and cognac for some of the men on our journey, we drove to a remote corner of Calais where we were parted from the Citroen which was to travel somewhere in the murk behind us, on the night car-train to Nice.

"Oh dear, I do hope our suitcases will be alright!" I bleated, as a youth in shiny yellow rain-gear seized the keys from Dick and ordered us to repose ourselves inside a grimy waiting-room till our train was announced.

It was a long dreary wait surrounded by po-faced English couples going on their Easter holidays to St Tropez or Portofino.

"Where are you two planning to spend your holidays?" inquired a stout lady wearing tweeds the colour of horse manure, with sensible shoes to match.

"A few days in Italy, then we're crossing from Ancona to Split," I told her.

"Split? Isn't that in Bosnia, where all the fighting is going on? You must be mad!"

"No, it's in Croatia, several miles away from the Bosnian border. And we're not going on holiday; we're going to see some old friends out there who are having a very tough time..."

Embarkation on the train was announced at that moment. "Just as well," Dick remarked; "before you start getting too argumentative!"

The *wagon-lits* carriage rumbled through the night and I lay awake in my bunk wondering how the Citroen was getting on, somewhere way back in the dark landscape behind us? And whether we should be gassed in our bunks? Last year, I had been told, a number of *wagon-lits* travellers were quietly put to sleep with gas-bags held over their faces, while a gang of thieves stole all their money and everything of value they possessed.

It was dawn before I fell asleep, and soon afterwards the train came to a grinding halt. I was in the middle of cooking a large rabbit in a very small saucepan when I awoke with a start and pulled the blind a few inches away from the window ... and there was a tall primrose-yellow building bathed in a gentle spring sunrise and, just below it, in line with my eyes, stood a board announcing MARSEILLE St CHARLES. On the far side of the building I could see a wedge of cornflower-blue sky and, simultaneously, the heady aroma of Gauloise cigarettes, crushed garlic and sunkissed leather came seeping through the window.

That was the moment when I knew there was no turning back. We had survived the first night, Marseille saluted us at daybreak and two and a half weeks of unknown adventures lay ahead.

*   *   *   *   *   *

The first four days were not very inspiring. We drove east from Nice through the Alpes Maritimes and the Ligurian Alps – no longer over the mountains on one of those glorious Corniches I remembered from journeys with my parents, but through a series of long, dark tunnels: headlights on, dripping water from the dank walls and ceiling, yellow continental lights coming towards us, then a few brief intervals in the daylight. But the mountains were covered with glass-houses – perhaps early tomatoes, peaches or grapes? And the Riveria towns with all those beautiful names – Bordighera, San Remo, Alassio – were linked together, a never-ending chain of buildings, great and small.

We met the rush-hour traffic pouring out of La Spezia, then Florence, in the late afternoon. Hundreds of cars travelling at top speed with loud horns and aggressive sallow-faced men behind their wheels. The endless suburban sprawl west of the city engulfed us, and the little village of Artimino was nowhere to be found.

"I can't believe it," Dick sighed. "I thought this was meant to be the famous Tuscan landscape, the paradise of English poets and authors?"

"Perhaps it'll get better when we approach the mountains," I offered hopefully.

Artimino, when we eventually found it, was perfect. An exquisite old village perched on a hill-top with the Hotel Paggeria Medicea crowning a neighbouring summit. We spent a marvellously comfortable and luxurious night there and awoke refreshed to the sound of the Tuscan birds singing their hearts out among the cypresses. The fifteen suitcases still reposed unmolested in the back of the Citroen, and we drove away towards the backbone of Italy with the sun beating down on the roof of the car.

The mountains beyond Arezzo were beige-coloured and rather shabby – nothing like the snow-capped giants filled with bandits of which I had dreamt. We zigzagged up the western flanks and had a picnic lunch on the pass, surrounded by last year's beer cans and plastic remnants. A large inquisitive man suddenly appeared over the brow of the hill and demanded a detailed account of our plans: "Where are you going? Where do you intend to stay when you get there? For how many nights? Then where will you go?"

Dick smiled amiably and offered him some olives, and I said quite firmly; "We are going to Croatia," which caused him to gulp and stare at us with round incredulous eyes.

The east side of the backbone of Italy was better. Fewer cars and scattered villas, more spring flowers and a prettier landscape. We had planned a short holiday at Urbino, the famous Renaissance town among the hills of Marche within a few miles of the Adriatic coast – a breathing-space and a short rest before the serious part of our journey began.

Urbino was certainly a gem of a walled town with its fifteenth century fortress and the distant vista of turrets and cupolas; the ancient archways leading through the walls to the Duke's Palace, the monastery, several exquisite churches and the house where Raphael was born. But our three night pause there was too long.

I suppose we were geared up by then to facing another kind of world – a brutal civil war taking place along the fringes of our dream islands – and Italy proved to be too self-satisfied and sophisticated, too busy sorting out her own dishonest politicians, making money from the tourists and drawing her skirts away from the grim facts of life on the other side of the Adriatic Sea.

*   *   *   *   *   *

We had brought the fifteen suitcases upstairs to our bedroom for our stay in Urbino, and they caused a good deal of interest among the staff and guests when we trundled them back through the hotel foyer and out to the car on the morning of our departure.

"I shan't be sorry to start emptying some of these," Dick declared with feeling, as he locked the padlock securing the heavy chain and covered the whole ensemble with a rough piece of canvas.

The early spring sun shone warmly on the hills of Marche as we drove eastwards to Fano, where we stopped for lunch, then on through Senigallia beside the placid blue waters of the Adriatic Sea.

"We're going to reach Ancona at least four hours too early," I predicted, as we sped along the coastal road towards the south.

"Never mind; far better than having a frantic last minute rush!" Dick grinned, treading fiercely on the accelerator.

It was March 28th, the day of the opening of the "I Dream of Peace" Exhibition in London, and I tried to visualize our Croatian friends travelling south in their coach, all wearing their best clothes and feeling very excited at the thought of meeting the television stars and Martin Bell; and the children picturing themselves as mini-stars for that one special day in their lives.

The coast ahead of us curved round in a wide sweep towards the south-east, culminating in a bold headland and a lighthouse on the end of a long jetty. As we drew nearer I could see the funnels and masts of ships, with black smoke drifting up into the gentle blue sky. There was no need to ask the way to the dock area as it beckoned to us from far away. We drove past a ship-building yard with big white hangars and a gantry that seemed to touch the sky; and, finally, we drew up outside an ugly building which combined ticket office, passport control, customs and immigration under one roof. A van pulled up beside us with *"Médecins sans Frontières"*

Marijana and Natali in the coach going to London on March 28th, 1994.

The "I Dream of Peace" exhibition at the Imperial War Museum - March 1994. Ivan with Vanessa Redgrave, the little boy from Sarajevo who lost an eye, two friends of his and Damir.

Photo: Courtesy of Daily Telegraph

inscribed on its sides, and I noticed a very small nun step out of a black car with Roman registration numbers and walk briskly towards the building.

All the doors were closed, and a dock-worker lounging on a bollard growled something about the hour of the siesta when I asked him what time they were due to reopen. We locked the car and went for a stroll round the back of the building, and there we found our ship. She was quite small and white, her name was ISTRA and she looked rather battered. Many of her portholes were filled in – like the windows of houses after the window-tax came into effect.

"I suppose that's to stop the bullets getting inside the ship?" I suggested, but Dick only grunted and moved away to examine some immense lorries with INTERNATIONAL TRANSPORT KARKANAKIS picked out in large black letters along their sides.

Beyond the custom-house and car-park rose a range of tall melon-coloured buildings with a church overlooking them which had a pale blue dome. And beyond that a steep slope of dark green trees culminated in the cathedral of Ancona – high up on top of the promontory.

"I like this place; it looks like the last outpost in Italy!" I said to no one in particular, as Dick was already striding back towards the custom-house where a door had just opened. A swarm of muscular men were trying to push their way inside – like a fat cork being rammed into a wine bottle.

The interior was filled with noise and the smell of coarse tobacco and cheap red wine. Groups of rough-looking, unshaven men struggled with each other to reach the window of the ticket office behind which sat a stern-faced woman flanked by computers. The tiny nun joined the queue of travellers close beside us, as well as a Swiss couple whose eyes shone with religious fervour.

"Doubtless you are travelling to Medjugorije for the Easter celebrations?" the lady asked me in German.

"No, we are going to Brač and Hvar Islands," I told her, remembering what I had read about the place in Bosnia-Hercegovina where the Virgin Mary made a miraculous appearance to some children in 1981, and reappeared from time to time to draw the coachloads of pilgrims into town. But it had recently become a hive full of honey for the Black Marketeers catering for the thugs dressed in flashy Italian clothes and their pouting girlfriends who drove up there in stolen cars to visit the well-stocked shops and sleazy discothéques.

The Swiss lady regarded us with disapproval, but relented when I explained that we were not tourists, but hoping to take 'aid' to some old friends on the islands and in Istria.

The press of ruffians had become worse than ever by that time, and the Swiss lady's husband told us they were a mixture of Albanians trying to return to their own country, and Spaniards driving big lorries filled with 'aid' for Bosnia. After a petrifying hour or two in the middle of the scrum, we finally received our boarding tickets for the ISTRA, leaving at 8 pm., and passed through the custom-house and passport control. The Roman nun was just behind us in the queue, and I was amazed by the sweetness of her expression and the calm acceptance of her surroundings inside that hell-hole.

Back in the Citroen, we still had an hour to wait before embarkation was due to start. We ate a quick snack in the café across the road, then drove out of the car-park and placed ourselves in what seemed the most strategic position for driving up the ramp and into the ship. Other people were beginning to have the same idea, and all around us swarmed restive lorries, transit vans and mini-buses, jockeying for superior positions from which to charge the ISTRA's ramp when the moment came. Many of the Spanish vehicles had the names of famous Bosnian battle zones like Tuzla, Travnik, Vitez, Goražde and Sarajevo painted in proud letters on their sides, and their drivers looked young and carefree, and not nearly as villainous as they had seemed inside the custom-house.

The early spring twilight crept imperceptibly over the restless scene; meanwhile more and more lorries came rumbling into town.

"I wonder if they all have bookings on our ship?" I asked Dick anxiously; "or are they just turning up on the off chance of getting aboard?"

"No way of telling," he grunted peevishly. "But if we have too much trouble getting aboard, I shall get to hell out of here and drive straight back to England!"

With only twenty minutes to go before sailing time, a quartermaster ambled down the ramp wiping his dinner from the corners of his mouth with powerful oily hands, and removed the barrier. There was no question of beckoning cars aboard in orderly lines, according to which ones had arrived first. He just turned round and walked back up the ramp while the biggest lorries surged forward, completely blocking the way for any hopeful small fry.

We sat there frozen to our seats, unable to move an inch. I kept on sending up a silent prayer to the Almighty to keep a tiny space for us amid that thundering turmoil on the car-deck; and the driver of *"Médecins sans Frontières"* squeezed next to us, threw out his arms in a Gallic gesture and smiled at Dick as his shoulders rose to the level of his ears.

At one minute to eight a harsh-featured seaman came down the ramp and beckoned to us to follow him. There were still a great many lorries, vans and mini-buses champing at the bit to one side of us, but that man had the presence of a sergeant-major and no one dared move without his permission. The Citroen looked like a white mouse wedged in the middle of a herd of elephants; but what did it matter when there was just enough room to open one door and crawl out and, glory be to God, I could feel a big engine throbbing beneath the steel deck on which I stood.

*   *   *   *   *   *

The night of March 28th was clear and tranquil – the night after the full moon with a silver runway spreading out from the starboard side of the ship to some invisible point in eternity. After all the traumas of embarkation, it seemed so strange to be ordering a meal in a pleasant dining-saloon and watching the lighthouses on the ends of the two moles flashing green to the north and red to the south, as they slid silently past the occasional unblocked portholes. I felt a sudden surge of excitement because we were at last under way, heading straight towards Croatia; and Dick, simultaneously, ordered a bottle of our favourite wine from Mostar with which to drink a toast to our journey.

The dinner was excellent and we had an outside cabin with two bunks, one above the other, with a porthole beside the upper bunk. Dick said he was tired and was not interested in looking out of the porthole, so I could have the upper bunk. He soon fell asleep and I suppose I would have done the same under normal circumstances; but there was nothing normal about our surroundings, so I sat up in bed with my nose pressed against the porthole all night long.

There was something quite magic about that passage across the Adriatic. The almost-full moon set in a star-studded sky shone down on a calm black sea, while the ship drove steadily eastwards, throwing up a phosphorescent bow-wave to vie with the glory of the sky above her.

Somewhere around 2 a.m. I saw a light flashing on the starboard beam and thought it must come from Palagruža, a tiny island in mid-Adriatic. Soon, however, the powerful shape of a NATO warship loomed up to the south of us, and the flashing light suddenly became a blinding Aldis lamp directed at our bridge. The ISTRA slowed down for a few minutes, then gathered speed again and continued on her way.

I must have fallen asleep shortly before dawn, because I woke with a start and saw that it was getting light outside. Already there was a rosy glow in the eastern sky and the dark outline of an island beneath it.

I grabbed some clothes and slid silently down the ladder from the top bunk. Dick slept on, his breathing as regular as a baby's. I crept out of the cabin and found a staircase leading to the top deck. It was marvellous up there, alone with the moon and the daybreak, and the sun about to rise over the mountains of Bosnia. We were entering the Splitska Vrata (the doorway to Split), and the dark tree-clad hills rose straight up from sea-level on either side of the ship – the hills of Šolta and Brač Islands.

I could just make out the whereabouts of our favourite cove on the north-west corner of Brač. A humpy grey rock hid the entrance, but I knew that an idyllic anchorage lay behind it, at the head of a sharp bend to the north where a stone cottage clung to the hillside above and a ruined mansion stood on the east shore. It had a two-storeyed tower with a tiled roof at one end, but the rest of the house was open to the sky. I remembered the tall pink roses climbing up the inside walls to run riot along the jagged edges where the roof had once reposed. Bumble-bees buzzed in and out of the empty windows and the old house drowsed serenely under the warm Dalmatian sun. The water in the cove was usually transparent – a dazzling pool filled with emeralds and sapphires – when we rowed ashore to wander among the ruins, then climb the steep hill that was covered with cypresses, olive trees, rock-roses, thyme, rosemary and a thousand little flowers sprouting triumphantly from every rocky crevice.

Stipanska Cove

There was a splendid view of the anchorage from outside the old cottage where a stone table and seats would beckon to us from the shade of a fig tree. Above the door of the house was a carved emblem of two doves meeting, with the legend "RADOLFINAN - 1902" below it; and some

The stone doves above the door lintel at Radolfinan's house.

words had been painted on the front wall that I translated as meaning "Do not come here with evil in your heart".

I sometimes tried to picture the people who had once lived in that lovely place? The hills were a symphony of bird-song and the droning of busy insects and, although there was never anyone else in sight, we used to feel that we had joined a select company of specially fortunate people extending way back through the ages, who had also known the magic of Stipanska Cove.

I stared over my right shoulder at the fast receding shore, longing to know if Stipanska was still the same ... Dick stood beside me a moment later, pointing out the rugged limestone mountains on the mainland and the great city of Split floating in a peach-coloured haze. Gradually the details began to emerge: fingers of white apartment blocks to the east, the hump of the Marjan Peninsula to the west, the sturdy green lighthouse on the harbour entrance, a ferry-boat crossing our path, making for Šolta; then the outer walls of Diocletian's Palace with its tall cathedral presiding over a cluster of red-tiled roofs, honey-coloured buildings and motionless palm trees.

The foreground was painted in shades of blue and gold with a backdrop of purple hills behind it – very peaceful it all looked until a helicopter came roaring over the mountains from Bosnia, rapidly losing height as it made for the hospital landing-pad.

Chapter 17 - Dalmatia

We drove off the ISTRA's car-deck surrounded by giant Spanish lorries bound for Bosnia. No wild stampede to be first on the ramp that morning, as there were plenty of granite-jawed policemen to control the movements of every vehicle that emerged from the ISTRA's cavernous belly.

"*Dobar dan!*" one of them greeted us with a flicker of a smile when he saw the English numberplates. "You will please to join queue at side of custom-house."

We bared our teeth enthusiastically, but I noticed his automatic bulging in its holster and Dick muttered as he pulled ahead; "This is the big moment we've been dreading! I wonder what they'll say when they see what's under our canvas cover at the back?"

"I expect they've got plenty to keep them busy without bothering too much about such small fry as us," I offered hopefully.

Half an hour later I was beginning to bleat about my breakfast, or total absence of it, when we found we had reached the head of the queue. A man in a grey-green uniform with neurotic eyes and sternly-chiselled lips beckoned us forward and fired a round of staccato orders and questions at us: "Please to open the back of your car. Where are you going and for what purpose? How long do you intend to stay in Croatia? What have you got to declare? You will open this, that and the black suitcase ..."

I pulled out our overnight bags and unzipped them as a preliminary gesture, then removed the canvas cover; but at that point Dick, who was in a state of considerable nervous tension, pushed the key into the padlock securing our chain with such vigour that it refused to turn to the right or left or to withdraw itself from the lock, which caused a most unexpected setback.

Our man glared angrily at my husband while I tried to explain in my mediocre Croatian that we had been compelled to use this chain because of our journey across Italy – he knew, without doubt, what the Italians were like? He nodded with comprehension. Well, this was the lamentable result – I attempted a weak giggle – fifteen suitcases chained together that refused to be parted! But here – I produced my master-stroke from inside my handbag – were complete lists of the contents of each suitcase.

The lists were, of course, in English, but I began to translate them with the help of my dictionary. Out of the corner of one eye I could see the man shuffling his feet impatiently, and scowling at the transit van behind us which was revving up its engine in a threatening manner.

"O.K., O.K.," he suddenly exclaimed. "You go. *Do vidjenja i sretan put* (Goodbye and good journey)."

We threw our overnight bags back into the car, slammed the doors shut and, with a feeling of gratitude and amazement, drove past the armed sentries at the dock gates and out into the sunlit city of Split.

*   *   *   *   *   *

A press of hungry faces peered into the car until we had left the dock area and found ourselves driving past the big open market outside the eastern entrance to Diocletian's palace. Gone were the stalls of carved wooden souvenirs, crochet-work, toys, etc., to be replaced by acres of vegetables, boots and cheap clothing. But the early spring sunshine shone down on the stall-holders, and the musical thunder of Dalmatian voices reached us from across the wide boulevard.

Following our street map of Split, we were soon speeding along the main highway leading east. Tall white blocks of flats on either side, purple

An EC Monitor's car outside the Hotel Split.

A helicopter coming in to land at Split Hospital with wounded from Bosnia.

mountains to the left and the calm blue sea to the right; helicopters constantly taking off or coming in to land – we were approaching the huge hospital complex – and a medley of white EC Monitor's vans, jeeps driven at high speed by wild-eyed soldiers and small Italian cars kept us company along the 4-lane road.

We soon reached the Hotel Split and parked at the top of the hill above it, as there was an armed sentry guarding a barrier across the drive leading down to the front entrance. The mention of Ewen Southby-Tailyour's name, however, immediately produced an EC interpreter who was expecting our arrival and ushered our car through the barrier and down the hill; he then found us a trolley on which to unload ten of our famous suitcases.

A few minutes later Ewen, clad in white with a sunburned face and a pioneering look in his eyes – quite different from the rather sombre figure I remembered meeting at the In and Out Club in Piccadilly – welcomed us to Room 507 and showed no signs of flinching when our trolley was wheeled in behind us.

"We'll stow this little pile over in the corner on the far side of the bed," he instructed the porter. "And now let me introduce you to Fergus Marshall who will take you down to the bar, as I'm sure you'd like a cup of coffee? And I'll join you there in a few minutes."

The Hotel Split was a modern multi-storeyed block, and there was no way of making the lift stop at the floor on which the EC Monitors were lodged unless you had some magic pass-number. On that first visit Fergus, a charming Irish Colonel, steered us swiftly back to the ground floor explaining, meanwhile, that Ewen had an appointment at ten o'clock with the new young French diplomat who was taking over command of all the EC Monitors; and it seemed unlikely to prove a happy relationship!

Ewen joined us a few minutes later and confirmed what Fergus had told us. We had a quick cup of coffee together and arranged to meet for dinner on March 31st, the day we had planned to leave Brač and spend the night in Split. The interpreter reappeared to escort us past the sentry at the top of the hill. He was a very agreeable man, but I could not help wondering how accurate his translations would be when some important dialogue was taking place between an EC Monitor and a Serb, Croat or Bosnian leader? Would he be biased, or was he strictly neutral?

We drove back to the ferry terminal and sat in a queue of cars bound for Supetar, the main port on Brač Island. We intended to spend the first night in a hotel at Bol on the far side of the island, and the second one with Maté and Vera, our old friends who used to run a *gostionica* in the lovely village of Splitska. They had invited us for a much longer stay, but we judged that it would be a great strain for them to feed us, even for one night.

$$* \quad * \quad * \quad * \quad * \quad *$$

The crossing of the Brački Kanal took just over an hour. Very peaceful it was, sitting on deck in the sunshine eating salami sandwiches and watching the grey mountains on the mainland recede and the wooded coastline of Brač draw nearer.

A Dalmatian fisherman mending his nets.

Supetar is an attractive town built round a small harbour. It looked quite different from the last time we had seen it, three years ago: not a yacht or tourist in sight, the harbour filled with fishing-boats and sun-tanned fishermen mending their nets or peering into their engines. All the tourist shops were closed and the food shops had little to offer, apart from potatoes and green vegetables. There were many thin, pale-faced women and children wandering about the streets or stringing up lines of multi-coloured washing along the balconies in the big hotel complex to the west of the town; and the harbour cafés were filled with shabbily-dressed men, some looking sad and listless while others appeared furtive and conspiratorial. Perhaps they were not very successful Black Marketeers who had crossed from the mainland to sell their remaining goods in Supetar?

We drove out of town and followed the winding road that leads across the mountainous plateau to the south coast. Brač is the third largest of the Adriatic Islands, and its history goes back to the Stone, Bronze and Iron Ages. Farmers have found flint scrapers, knives, arrow-heads and tools from those periods – also the remains of ancient fortifications and burial grounds among the hills. All the early settlements were located inland because of the pirate's raids along the coast; and it was not until the Venetian settlers arrived in the fifteenth century that the people of Brač were able to move down to the coast and make contact with the neighbouring islands.

There were no other cars on the road and, so far, none of the villainous refugees about whom we had been warned by the Italian. But a pair of armed policemen waved us down as we approached the junction with a road coming up from the west coast.

"Halt! One is not permitted to travel on this road. Where are you making for?" asked the head policeman, who had suspicious eyes partially concealed beneath heavy lids and a face touched with gloom and frustration.

"To Bol," we told him. "We are going there for just one night because it is the only place with a hotel open on the whole island, we understand."

"Show me papers," he demanded. "You are tourists?"

"Yes!" I made a big effort to smile sweetly, remembering what Ewen had told us about their desperate wish to attract tourists back to Dalmatia.

Dick, meanwhile, rootled among the chaos in the back of the car but failed to find any suitable documents. The policeman stamped his feet irritably for some minutes then, scowling fiercely, he snarled; "O.K., you go. But tomorrow you come back, understood?"

We jumped back into the Citroen and got under way. I quickly shut my window as Dick was beginning to mutter "Officious little creep! Never said which papers – just stood there demanding PAPERS!"

We wound our way uphill towards Nerežišća, the eight-hundred-year-old village once considered the metropolis of Brač. All around us were olive groves, lavender fields, small vineyards surrounded by grey stone walls and the curious oval-shaped rain-water cisterns that supplied the neighbourhood with its drinking-water. Further on we could see the summit of Vidova Gora, the highest mountain in the Dalmatian Islands, and away to the north-east the red-tiled roofs of Pučišća, centre of the famous Brač stone quarries. The creamy-white stone was used to build Diocletian's palace in Split, the White House in Washington, the Canadian War Memorial at Vimy Ridge and Tito sent a block of it to England for Winston Churchill's statue by the Jugoslav sculptor, Oscar Nemon.

Our road looped over the mountainous spine of Brač near the hamlet of Gornji Humac, when suddenly we spotted the new airfield – small and inconspicuous at the end of a dirt track, with no sign to announce its presence to the outside world. The scenery began to change dramatically: no more Austrian pines nor holm-oaks; instead we were faced with the sun-baked maquis of the southern slopes, the sapphire-blue sea and the long island of Hvar across the straits; and, close at hand, some caves with gaping black mouths, each one big enough to house a family of bears.

Bol harbour on Brač Island.

Far below us lay the beautiful village of Bol, the spire of its Dominican monastery dominating a small peninsula to the east of the harbour and a necklace of vineyards encircling its landward side. Bol is a glorious place filled with ancient houses built of Brač stone. With the blue sky above them, the old wooden fishing-boats reflected in the emerald-green water, not a tourist in sight and the hum of Dalmatian voices coming from a café on the waterfront, it seemed a far cry from the horrors taking place in Bosnia, only a few miles away as the crow flies.

The Hotel Kastil received us with pleasure. We were, I believe, their only guests, apart from a few people dining under a canopy of vine leaves on the terrace overlooking the sea. We joined them as soon as we had washed and changed, and sat there in the twilight gazing at the little lighthouse on the end of the mole flashing green every three seconds, and the mountains of Hvar growing darker and more mysterious while the long purple shadows crept steadily towards us across the calm moonstone sea.

A fisherman bent over his net, attempting to mend it by the light of a dim paraffin lamp placed on the stern sheets of his boat; and two women stood by the wall just below our table, discussing the chances of a good crop of vegetables that spring and the shortage of firewood in the valley leading up to Vidova Gora.

A friendly waiter brought us 'cevapčiči sa lukom', a delicious dish of minced meat and herbs shaped like sausages and served with onions and a green salad. He lingered for a while to consider our plans and to share with us his thoughts on the course of the war in Bosnia.

"U.N. soldiers no damn good," he declared. "Make parley with Serb bastards, chase our girls, get drunk every night ... send them back home, best thing!"

We strolled along the waterfront after our meal and watched the moon rise magically from behind the distant mountains. A voice began to sing one of those hauntingly sad Dalmatian folk-songs in a room above the post-office, and suddenly we knew that Bol had stepped right back into its past – a village where the people worked endlessly to scratch a humble living out of the sea and the barren mountainside, until such time as the package tours, the tripper-boats and the aeroplanes from Northern Europe brought back the semi-nude tourists to violate their idyllic home.

*   *   *   *.   *   *

Next day was like the first day in creation. A shimmering silver pathway danced across the pale blue sea, all the way from our lighthouse to Rabbit Island off Hvar; the sky was a much deeper cornflower-blue, and the red-tiled roofs above the primrose-yellow stone houses with their carved Venetian balconies and elegant windows transformed the village into a dream come true.

After a breakfast of coffee, fresh rolls and scrambled eggs, we left the Hotel Kastil and paid a visit to the bank to change some traveller's cheques before driving back across the island.

"Do you know a *Gospoda* Cvitanić?" I asked the lady who handed me my Croatian dinars. "She and her family used to live in a little house outside Bol, at the foot of Vidova Gora." I showed her an old photograph of the young mother with her four children sitting on a wall, with a mountain rearing up behind them. It was taken some twenty-four years ago.

"Oh, yes! We know the family well. They live in the village now, and she has some grandchildren! Shall I tell them you are here? Look, Nadja, Jelena. Is it not a miracle?"

The other clerks in the bank had crowded round her, their eyes round and shiny as they peered at my old photograph and chattered about the children's appearance all those years ago.

Dick and I had decided to climb Vidova Gora during our first visit to Bol. It was a long hard scramble up a steep and slippery goat's track, and we collapsed on to a rock to rest and cool down after the first two or three hours. I shed my jersey and we shared a bottle of beer, then continued on our way; but it was not until we were hit by a freezing north wind near the summit of the mountain that I realized I had left my jersey behind on the rock. Dick gallantly draped his jacket around me while I assured him, "It won't be for long, as we'll soon get back to the place where I left it."

We stood among the thistles and wild thyme, transfixed by the grandeur of our position. Hvar, Korčula and distant Vis spread out like islands on a map away to the south, a grey stone cairn blended with the eternal grey rocks around us and the limestone giants on the mainland strode across the northern sky.

The jersey – a special favourite of mine – had gone by the time we reached our resting-place on the way back. Dick insisted that I should keep his jacket, but we both felt sad and disillusioned all the way down that mountain track, as we found it so hard to imagine a thief in our beloved Dalmatia. At last we came to a small lonely house – the first outpost of humanity on the lower slopes of Vidova Gora.

A woman stood at the gate – she seemed to be expecting us – and asked with a smile; "You will please come into my house and take a glass of wine?"

We followed her into a tiny white-washed kitchen, and she indicated two chairs and fetched a bottle of wine and a plate of cheese.

"Živeli!" we said, raising our glasses to that lovely lady and her four children who came running into the house to observe us.

She opened a drawer in the oak chest behind her and pulled out my jersey, which had been carefully folded and wrapped up in a newspaper.

"A man who came from *gore* (high up) on his donkey," she waved her arms dramatically towards the mountain, "passed here some hours ago and gave me this jersey to guard, as he felt sure that you would pass my home on your return journey!"

With my faith restored and my jersey clutched in my grateful hands, I knew that I should never forget *Gospoda* Cvitanić and the man with a donkey whom we never met. There was no time to renew our brief acquaintanceship that morning, but I wrote a message on the back of her photograph and left it with the lady in the bank.

We drove up the zigzag mountain road away from Bol, pausing for a few minutes at the hamlet of Murvica to make sure that the abandoned monastery of Draševa Luka still clung to the mountain face – a place filled with wild flowers, bumble bees, lizards ... and infinite peace. I picked a few violets, cowslips and tiny pink flowers (campions, I think), then we drove on across the spine of Brač. No policemen greeted us at the road junction, and we reached the shops at Supetar in time to buy a whole ham as an extra offering for Vera and Maté.

We had a picnic on the foreshore in order not to arrive at any time they might construe as lunchtime, then we paddled in the rock pools, watched the ferries and coasters crossing the Brački Kanal and, finally, drove east along the coast road to the ancient village of Splitska.

Chapter 18 - Our Old Friends

Vera stood half-way up the hillside, on the terrace outside her kitchen, with her arms held wide open and a big smile on her face.

"Where hast thou been all this time?" she called down to us. "I sent Jakše to Supetar to meet the morning boat from Split, but not a glimpse of my dear friends from England did he catch!"

Dick and I came panting up the steep stone staircase from harbour level – past the old crone's house where Maté's mother used to live; then to the second level, filled with flower-pots and climbing roses; and, finally, up to the third level and into Vera's arms.

No use lying to Vera, I could tell from the gleam in her eyes. "We crossed late last evening and did not wish to disturb you," I began, but I was saved from further explanations by Maté stepping out of the kitchen and sweeping us into his arms.

"*Dobro došli! Dobro došli!*" he exclaimed. Then Jakše, his wife, Ružica, and little Verica appeared, and Jakše went down to the car with Dick to help him haul our heavy suitcases up the steps.

Built round a deep cove on the north coast of Brač, the village of Splitska had scarcely changed since our first visit there twenty-two years ago. The fifteenth century Renaissance castle and parish church stood serenely indifferent to the passage of time near the head of the cove, and the lovely melon-coloured houses with their green shutters and tiled roofs rose tier upon tier up the eastern hillside, with an explosion of bougainvillaea, climbing roses, orange and lemon trees, honeysuckle, oleanders, and small palm trees occupying the foreground and all the gaps between the houses. A traveller arriving from Supetar just before sunset would see a perfect reflection of the village in the still waters of the cove – an idyllic dream hovering on the brink of the brutal war being waged on the far side of the Brački Kanal, a mere five miles to the mainland, then over the Dinaric Alps and into Bosnia.

"Jakše is home on leave for two weeks," Vera told us, as she filled some

The old church at Splitska.

tiny cups with Turkish coffee. "He has been defending the Maslenica Bridge near Zadar, thou knowest? It is very dangerous there, with shells landing around their encampment every day."

She shuddered as though a blast of icy wind had hit her, and I suddenly became aware of the changes the war had wrought in this family. Vera, her daughter-in-law, Ružica, and granddaughter, Verica, were literally starving. They had been living on little else but poor quality bread and potatoes for nearly two years by then, the vegetable crop having failed the previous summer because of the terrible drought; and Maté had been forced to sell their boat so they no longer had the chance to catch their own fish. Vera was in constant pain and could hardly stand or walk a few paces because of her hip that badly needed an operation; but that was out of the question with all the surgeons in Split so busy attending to the war casualties arriving daily from Bosnia.

Ružica was so thin and pale, she seemed like the ghost of the pretty young bride from Pučišća we had first met in 1984, and little Verica had hardly grown at all in the last few years; at nine she was the same size as her cousin, a plump boy of five.

Maté now had grey hair and a grey beard, but he looked the same Dalmatian father-figure we had always known; and Jakše, with his army rations, was clearly well-nourished and strong. He showed us with pride some photographs of himself taken by another soldier near the Maslenica Bridge, and invited us to choose the one we liked best.

"It is very hard for some families like us to exist any longer," Maté explained to us later on. "If you own your home, the government gives you no money on which to live; just a small food allowance once a month for each member of your family – it lasts for three or four days at the most – and there are no tourists who come here now and no work to be found. We rely entirely on a few vines and our vegetable patch, but when we have a bad season like last year there is nothing to eat or sell ... nothing at all."

He spread out his hands in a gesture of despair but Vera, meanwhile, was indulging in sharp intakes of breath and noises like the clucking of a contented hen as she unpacked our suitcases.

"Just look at that, Ruže!" she exclaimed excitedly. "A whole ham and all this lovely cheese and olive oil; and pills to stop my pains and a party blouse for Verice. And this skirt and jacket I shall wear for Mass on Easter Sunday."

The shoes we had brought for Ružica had one shoe of Size 7 and the other of Size 5! The pairs to each were clearly sitting in another suitcase in Ewen's bedroom at the Hotel Split. I tried to explain what had happened without revealing that we had a number of other families to visit, and promised to send her the pair to Size 5 in a few days' time.

Jakše and Ružica, whose flat was on a terrace higher up the hillside, had prepared their own bedroom for us to sleep in – a lovely room with a view over the roof-tops and palm trees of Splitska to the Brački Kanal and the mountains on the mainland.

"We hope you will be comfortable and stay with us for many days," Ružica said as she left us. "Tonight Vera and I prepare a special dinner for you, and tomorrow I will show you my new kitchen and sitting-room."

We walked to the little lighthouse at the entrance to the cove before dinner. It was flanked by miniature pine trees and a few modern villas, and we sat on the rocks watching an oil tanker flying the Maltese flag being escorted through the straits by a Norwegian destroyer – part of the NATO Operation Sharp Guard.

Maté and Vera's daughter, Bosilka, and her husband and little boy came to dinner that evening – in fact, I think they brought part of the meal with them. We ate a delicious chicken stew, followed by langoustines with a

Jakše defending the Maslenica Bridge - Winter 1994.

green salad, and some special wine of Brač that Maté had been saving for our visit. It was not until a few days later, when someone told us that each langoustine would have cost at least £5, that we realized the immense effort and sacrifice it must be for a family to entertain visitors. It was like a scene from the Bible watching our old friends seated round the kitchen table eating by candlelight and, in their hearts, giving thanks to God for all that unaccustomed food.

Dick raised his glass and said *"Živeli!"* Then we drank to a rapid end to the war, a plentiful harvest in 1994 and good health and happiness for our hosts. I asked Ružica about some of the books in our room: a set of Croatian classics and a beautiful illustrated book on Brač and its ancient history.

"I used to love reading," she told me; "and those are some of my favourite books."

I looked out of our window much later that night. There was a thin moon and many stars, the lights of ships steaming towards Split, the red flashing light on the corner of our cove and a wonderful scent of orange blossom wafting towards me on the night breeze.

* * * * * *

Vera appeared very distressed when we told her that we must catch the morning ferry back to Split.

"I expected thee for a week at least," she protested. "After travelling across half of Europe to visit us, thou canst not leave so soon?"

"We have only a very short holiday," I tried to explain; "and we have promised to visit our refugee friends near Rijeka on our way home."

She must surely have been relieved that we were not proposing to linger in Splitska, but we could see no signs of this in her woeful expression as she laid before us an immense breakfast of ham, eggs, cheese, freshly baked bread, local honey and coffee.

"At least the ham and cheese are from the supplies we brought them," I whispered to Dick as we helped ourselves as sparingly as possible, making copious excuses about not being used to eating anything for breakfast.

Earlier that morning Ružica had shown us their beautiful red and white kitchen and sitting-room, a present from Maté and Vera and the reason, we suspected, that Maté had been obliged to sell his boat. We wandered round the two rooms admiring this and that: a bowl and a small vase made of the exquisite creamy-white Brač marble, a table-cloth Vera had crocheted to lay on top of the larger red cloth covering their sitting-room table, the crimson kitchen utensils, so striking against the white walls.

"You must be very proud of your home," I told the girl, and her face lit up with a rare smile as she answered me in English – a big surprise as no one else in the family spoke any foreign language.

She confided that she had worked in a travel office some years ago, and had frequent opportunities to speak in our language in those days.

We went across to the little supermarket after

The Bašković family with Dick on their terrace at Splitska. Left to right: Ružica, Jakše, Vera and Verica, Dick, Maté and his grandson.

breakfast, to see if we could find a few extra useful presents before we left Splitska. The glasses were laid out for a farewell drink on the terrace when we returned, and Maté poured out the wine and presented us with the branch of a palm tree to take with us for Easter. Vera and Ružica, who had been missing, suddenly reappeared bearing five or six parcels wrapped up in white paper.

"You must not, you cannot give us all these presents!" I tried to protest, but Vera commanded me to be silent and put them in one of our empty suitcases and open them when we reached home – in that way we would not forget our old friends in Splitska.

We raised our glasses for the last toast and I blew my nose noisily to try and hide the tears pouring out of my eyes; but when I looked around I saw that everyone else had tears rolling down their cheeks – even Dick and Jakše.

The ferry from Supetar to Split was already warming up its engine as we drove on to the ramp, and I spotted our policeman from the road junction in the centre of Brač eyeing us suspiciously as we sped past him. Five minutes later we were under way, sitting on the port side of the upper deck so that we could no longer see little Splitska fading away into the distance behind us.

*　　　*　　　*　　　*　　　*　　　*

"We'd both like steak tartar," Fergus Marshall told the waiter, after an extensive examination of the menu. "That is if you are able to cook such a dish?"

The waiter gave him a long hard stare, wrote a few words on his note-pad and disappeared towards the kitchen. Ewen and Fergus were dining with us at the Split Yacht Club which had one of the few restaurants where they were allowed to eat in the city, apart from the Hotel Split where they lived. And the waiter was an old friend of theirs as they sometimes brought visiting politicians to dine there – Baroness Linda Chalker, the Minister for Overseas Development, had been their last guest, only a week ago.

A pair of glowering, sparsely-shaved men with an aura of the Balkan thug about them occupied the table next to ours. They were locked in urgent conversation – perhaps plotting some lucrative business deal – while devouring course after course of rich food without noticing its arrival or departure. I thought of Maté and Vera the previous night and I had a sudden desire to spit at them, so I turned away and pretended they did not exist.

Ewen, meanwhile, was telling Dick about his job as an EC Monitor, and the journeys he and Fergus made in their white Landrover along the frontier line in Krajina.

"There's a place called Knin a few miles inland from Šibenik," he said, "and there are quite a few trigger-happy soldiers on both sides of the line in that area. Hardly a house remains undamaged for miles around and atrocities happen every day, despite all the peace-keepers. There's one chap I know up there, in command of the Croatian soldiers along that part of the line. He's a serious-minded, decent sort of person, and he believes in keeping a firm grip on his men – no incidents allowed in his area at all. But he told me in private last time we were up there that he had a list of Serb names locked inside his desk; and if ever the time came when peace was declared he, personally, would kill with his own hands everyone on that list – and, afterwards, willingly take the consequences."

"Yes, the depths of hatred among some of those people who went to the same schools and grew up together is something we find hard to understand," Fergus confirmed.

A long pause in our conversation occurred when the waiter returned with the ingredients of the steaks tartar. He hung over the serving table like a magician, breathing strange incantations while he ground coarse salt and pepper over the chopped raw beef mixed with bone marrow, then gently shaped it into tournedos with wells in their centres into which he dropped the raw yolks of two eggs. With a sharp knife and fork he worked the egg yolks into the beef mixture, and added finely chopped onions, capers, anchovy fillets wrapped around stoned olives, and gherkins. Finally he included a sieved hard-boiled egg, some chopped parsley and a few drops of Worcester Sauce; then sculpted the whole affair back into the shapes of two steaks and transferred them on to clean plates.

The men on my right glanced briefly at this engrossing performance, then continued their conversation with renewed urgency.

"How did your interview go with the new French diplomat?" I asked Ewen during a pause, when the waiter had run back to the kitchen to fetch some new ingredients.

"Even worse than I had feared," he confided. "The little swine wants to give me a desk job, running our office in Zadar. I go home on leave for Easter and I may well decide to stay there, the way things are turning out."

Fergus declared that it was very sad for the EC Monitors to lose a man like Ewen, as his skills were out in the field communicating with people in a situation that was extremely explosive, and not sitting around in an office with shells raining down on top of him most of the time.

"I thought the coastal area was supposed to be fairly safe, until you get south of Dubrovnik?" Dick surmised.

"Oh, no. You don't read about it any more in the English newspapers, but places like Zadar, Vodice and Šibenik are being shelled, off and on, all the time. In fact, the Croat's biggest ammunition dump is right beside one of the more popular yacht harbours along the coast, and the Serbs up in the hills love having a go at that. But there's one thing I can tell you from experience," Ewen leaned forward and waved his fork encouragingly at Dick; "and that is that the chances of your being hit by a shell if you find yourself near the front line are really very small!"

Dick attempted a weak smile, the waiter announced that the steaks tartar were ready and another waiter brought our *ražnici*, a delicious dish of lamb cubes, peppers and onions grilled on skewers over a charcoal fire. Another bottle of the red wine of Mostar was ordered, then we all drank suitable toasts to each other to cover the next few weeks.

Later that night, back at the Hotel Split, we decided to open our parcels given us by Maté and Vera before we left Splitska. It was a heart-rending experience because we found inside them some of their most special treasures that we had admired in their home. There was, for instance, the little marble bowl and vase, and the beautiful crocheted table-cloth from Ružica's sitting-room; and six of the classics from behind our bed as well as the glorious illustrated book about the Island of Brač; and Maté had included a bottle of his precious wine and another of olive oil. It was all too clear what had happened: having no money to go out and buy us presents, they had given us some of the things we had admired most in their home. We felt like bursting into tears again as we gazed at one treasured gift after another.

*   *   *   *   *   *

Our room was on the sixth floor of the Hotel Split – one of the floors where the lift consented to stop. In order to retrieve our luggage from Ewen's room, he was obliged to trundle it down to Reception on the ground floor, where we met him and stacked it in the lift again to return to the sixth. Shortly afterwards he and Fergus left on their daily run up to the trouble spots in Krajina, and Dick and I sat on our balcony watching the aeroplanes and helicopters coming in low over the mountains every few minutes, to land at the hospital's airstrip.

Our balcony overlooked an annexe of the hotel in which lived families of refugees from Bosnia. I watched them hanging up their washing to dry in the spring sunshine, and I could see inside some of their sparsely-furnished rooms. I tried to picture how they must feel about their never-ending exile from any place they could call their own home, but this led to nostalgic thoughts about our own refugees and a strong desire to know how they were getting along.

We left the hotel about midday, with the back of the Citroen once more filled with suitcases. Dick drove swiftly across the city to Lučica Špinut, the small yacht harbour on the north side of the Marjan Peninsula where our old friend, Captain Maroje Maroević, was still in charge.

"I am glad to see that you have come to visit our city again," he greeted us, clasping our present of a bottle of malt whisky to his jersey like a mother might clasp her first-born child. "I wish you to take a message back to the Royal Cruising Club and to all your British yachtsmen."

That's a tall order, I thought to myself, while he continued to gaze joyously at the parcel in his arms.

"You are to tell them that they are to come to Croatia to sail this summer," he commanded us. "All is now normal, there are no dangers at all and they can sail everywhere!" His hands described wide circles to include the entire eastern half of the Adriatic Sea. "No more *problemas*, you understand?"

We nodded vigorously and stretched our faces into broad grins, refraining from telling him what Ewen had revealed the previous evening. Then we took photographs of the Captain at the end of the jetty, and told him that we must visit our friends aboard MINTHAMI as we believed they had just returned from England.

MINTHAMI, an ageing Eventide, a wooden sailing boat designed by Maurice Griffiths, stood on the quay-side with boxes of stores beneath her and all over her cabin-top and cockpit, while Paul and Sheila Morris tried to subdue their two-year-old son who was not convinced that he would like the confined space in which they would be living for the next few months.

I sat in the cabin talking to Sheila while Dick and Paul chatted in the cockpit. Chris, it transpired, was born an hour after MINTHAMI had crossed a minefield in 1992. It was a choice of waiting in some peaceful harbour, hoping there would be no complications, or making a dash for Split and its hospital despite the presence of mines in the approaches to Lučica Špinut! They decided to accept the risk of being blown up, and we were now being introduced to their firstborn child.

"I'm not sure that we'll be able to stay out here much longer, living aboard MINTHAMI," Paul confided to Dick. "A lot depends on how the youngster takes to the boat this summer."

We drove to the wooded Marjan Peninsula for a picnic lunch, then descended into the heart of Split, parked the car and I said a little prayer to ask for the protection of our remaining suitcases.

The interior of Diocletian's palace was quite different to what we remembered. There were neither tourists nor tourist shops to feed them; only a few rather empty kiosks and other premises displaying shabby garments, tough-looking footwear, do-it-yourself kits and some of the bare necessities of life, and cafés filled with soldiers on leave or men who were doing very nicely for themselves out of the war. It was some of the eyes that struck a chord of horror in my brain: those dark brown soulless eyes, without a glimmer of compassion or joy or laughter ... something had been extinguished inside those men and nothing they could do would ever rekindle the light. We drank coffee that tasted like wood at what was once our favourite café, then strolled past the wonderful Meštrović statue of Bishop Grgur of Nin outside the Golden Gate. The big toe of one of his sandalled feet is burnished bright because of the thousands of passers-by who cannot resist stroking it!

We bought some cassettes for Marijana by two of her favourite Croatian singers, Prljavo Kazalište and Zlatne Dukate, in the big department store outside the Golden Gate; then returned to the car – which had not been tampered with – and drove back to the port to catch the evening ferry to Hvar.

She came in on time – a dark silhouette against the brilliant evening sun – and her name was VANGA. She had a strict quartermaster in charge of loading.

"You will place your car here," he ordered Dick, indicating a position just behind the bow doors; "and in that way you will be the first ashore at Starigrad!"

We thanked him for his kindness, and climbed up to the top deck where the sky was yellow and black and a strong southerly wind was churning up the oily water inside the harbour.

$$* \quad * \quad * \quad * \quad * \quad *$$

The VANGA was full of families going home, or to visit their relatives, for Easter. There were small boys climbing up the ventilators and swinging from the cargo derricks, and a little girl who sat on a hatch-cover clasping a cardboard box to her body as if it contained the most precious thing in the world. Presently she opened a corner of the box to peer inside, but her anxious face was quickly pushed aside by the head of a large black and white rabbit! Two paws then appeared, but the child's mother arrived just in time to prevent the whole animal climbing out on to the hatch.

It was nearly dark as the ferry ploughed towards the Splitska Vrata against a rising gale. I could see a small fishing-boat, the outline of her

A small fishing-boat, her lateen sail outlined against the wooded mountains of Western Brač.

lateen sail etched against the wooded mountains of Western Brač; and, further on, the little green-flashing lighthouse on Mrduja Islet, standing guard at the approaches to the port of Milna. White-crested waves met the VANGA in the narrowest part of the straits, and the big lighthouse on Rt Ražanj lit up a fierce line of washing streaming out to leeward between the light-tower and the keeper's cottage – immense woollen bloomers, vests and shirts – as its powerful light swept over them every five seconds.

Dick and I retreated to the bar while the ferry crossed the angry waters of the Hvarski Kanal. It was filled with tobacco smoke and the resonant voices of Dalmatia: young soldiers going on leave, old men with stories to share with the barman and family groups whose shopping-bags were overflowing with treats from Split. We ordered some black coffee and sat by the window peering into the tumultuous night.

After an hour or so the sea grew calmer, and we steamed along the Starigradski Zaljev with an impression of tall mountains forming a lee on our starboard side. One more light, a fixed green one, on the outer end of the ferry-boat jetty, and the VANGA came to a gentle halt. Dim figures secured our ramp in position, and a few minutes later we drove ashore on to the Island of Hvar. The lady in the London travel office had told us there was only one hotel open on the island – all the others had been commandeered for refugees.

"I book you a room at the Hotel Mina in Jelsa," she informed us. "It is very modern nice hotel".

We turned left off the ferry-boat pier, and drove eastwards into the black night and pouring rain.

"I hope it's something like our hotel at Bol," I murmured. "Jelsa's only a small town so it shouldn't be too difficult to find."

Dick grunted pessimistically as he drove past the turning to Starigrad town and, a little further on, the road leading to Vrboska. I was wrong, because it was VERY difficult to find. We were both tired and we drove all round Jelsa harbour several times, asking people who were loitering on the waterfront if they knew which road we should take to the Hotel Mina. They gave conflicting advice – or perhaps my powers of translation were not at their best. Whatever the reason, it was a long time before we found ourselves driving up a steep zigzag road leading into the hills away from the town. Each time we saw someone Dick paused while I asked them if this was the right road to the hotel. And each time they smiled sympathetically and replied "*Da, da! Gore, gore* (Yes, yes! High up, high up)."

We ground to a halt at last outside an immense pile with only two lights showing. Dick parked the car and growled "Bugger the suitcases for tonight! If this is the right place we'll just take our night things in, and see to the others in the morning."

It was the Hotel Mina, all 450 rooms of it, but the receptionist greeted us cautiously, demanded our passports and told us we were their only *goste* (guests) at present! She handed us a key and I asked if we could have dinner as soon as we had left our bags upstairs.

"The restaurant is closed," she replied in a firm voice; "but I will ask my colleague if there is food to be had."

Her colleague, a sparsely-shaved man in a burgundy-red jacket, took pity on us, and he contrived to bring us a tray of ham and eggs some while later which we ate at a small table in the vast marble-floored entrance hall.

"We hope to have many guests in June this year," he predicted, hovering over us while we hungrily devoured our supper. "But this is the quiet season, you understand?"

Later that night we shivered in bed while the wind-devils howled among the black mountains of Hvar, and the rain beat a steady tattoo on the floor of our balcony.

"I hope the suitcases are alright," I murmured to Dick, before falling into a deep dreamless sleep.

Hvar is a long thin island with a mountainous spine running down the centre, and only one main road which starts in Hvar Town and climbs up through Brusje, then down again through Starigrad and Jelsa, and on and on to the far end of the island, some forty miles further east. Jelsa was first recorded as the fishing port of Pitve in Illyrian times, and the sea used to lap against the walls of the fourteenth century church of Sveti Ivan before the marshy land around the harbour was drained. An oval window with massive stone surrounds was built low down in the wall, so that fishermen could row in close to it to make their confessions, without being obliged to leave their boats. Nowadays there are wild flowers sprouting from the roof of the church, and a road ambles past the oval window where confessions are no longer heard.

We had booked for four nights at the Hotel Mina – a sobering thought next morning as the rain slashed across the windows and the mountains glowered dark and threatening above the little town.

We had breakfast in the restaurant surrounded by four hundred empty tables; but it was a good breakfast served by a friendly waiter. Later we went shopping to buy some last minute extras for Jakov and Matica, and succeeded in purchasing a sirloin of beef – about 50 Deutsch marks (or £20) on the Black Market. I persuaded our waiter to keep it in the hotel's refrigerator until the following morning.

The rain stopped around midday and long fat clouds like grey duvets with virgin-white surrounds hung about the mountain summits. We drove to Vrboska and strolled past the fortified church of Sveti Marija, then round the almost landlocked bay. I noticed that PARTIZAN III, the famous Partisan's boat which had always taken pride of place in the old boat-building yard since the end of the Second World War, had been removed.

We had a picnic lunch by the water's edge outside the Hotel Adriatic, a place filled with happy memories of a perfect spring holiday we had spent there some years ago. It was quite empty and silent – no refugees and no *gostes* – but there were hundreds of wild flowers under the pine trees and bees buzzing industriously among the lavender and rosemary bushes. And the recently-built nudist's camp was also quite empty.

We sat on the rocks and listened to our first 1994 cuckoo; then the sun came out and turned the cove into a dazzling diamond bracelet, and patches of blue sky appeared through the canopy of pine needles above us.

"It's beginning to feel more like Hvar every minute," I told Dick as we wandered back to the village and bought some food for our supper.

That night we lit our camping-stove in the bedroom and cooked *Goulash Jelsa* in a small saucepan. It tasted excellent, served with fresh bread and red wine of Hvar.

*   *   *   *   *   *

You could see for miles up on the ridge. Range upon range of rugged mountains over in Bosnia, fading away into a purple haze as they strode towards the borders of Montenegro. The great bulk of Brač crouched like a sleeping lion in the foreground and, nearer still, the little towns of Starigrad and Vrboska nestled among the vineyards and lavender fields beneath our feet. On the southern side the Pakleni Isles clung like children to the skirts of Mother Hvar and, far away on the distant horizon, the Island of Vis appeared like a moonstone set in a sea of aquamarines.

It was Easter Sunday, a glorious April symphony of a day, and we were picking rosemary and listening to the skylarks up on the ridge; also watching the time so that we did not arrive in Brusje too late. There were no others cars nor people in sight, just a crucifix by the side of the road which someone had decked with fresh spring flowers.

We drove into the village of Brusje twenty minutes later: grey stone houses with tiled roofs and green shutters, as old as the hills on which they stood; church bells ringing, a donkey tethered in a back yard and a big square-shaped figure striding towards us with wide open arms.

That was how we dreamt of Brusje when we were far away, and that was how it still was, that Easter morning. Dick and I jumped out of the car and Jakov enfolded us – first Dick, then me – in a bear's hug that made us gasp for breath.

Jakov and Dick singing "Vužgi" in the Dulčić family's kitchen in their house at Brusje.

"Welcome, my dearest friends!" he greeted us, his eyes alight with joy. "We have waited for you for three long years."

Matica stood in her kitchen like Mother Earth, with the kettle simmering on the stove and her special Easter cakes layed out on the table.

"Be seated and I will bring you coffee," she said, just as she had done that first time, twenty-six years ago.

Jakov opened a bottle of home-made *raki* and filled four glasses, then we sat around the table drinking toasts to one another and, presently, Jakov and Dick began to sing. First they sang *"Vužgi"*, about the magic world to be found on the other side of the mountains; and afterwards the song about the young soldier far from home, thinking of his mother in a peaceful village by the sea.

Matica and I, meanwhile, began to unpack the suitcases, and she let out exclamations of wonder and appreciation from time to time: *"Krasno! Prima! Ljepo! Bog čuvaš* (God protect thee), etcetera."

Jakov pretended not to notice, as he prefers to give and not receive; but Matica is a realist who receives with pleasure those things that are quite impossible for her to make or buy. The Size 7 shoes had been reunited and fitted her perfectly, so she danced around the kitchen to show us how they looked. "Today I wear them for church!" she proclaimed with great pride.

Both our friends looked older and thinner, and their hair had turned quite grey since we last saw them; but they were not starving like Vera and her family in Splitska, and they still held their heads high like the Partisans of old.

"There is one great sadness for Matica and me," Jakov told us; "and that is the way our government under President Tudjman tries to destroy the memory of Tito. They have cast away our old boat, PARTIZAN III – you must remember her in Vrboska? The museum and all the monuments in Vis where I helped to fight the Germans under your Colonel Fitzroy Maclean have all gone, and we ourselves dare not admit to being old Partisans any longer; and yet those were the proudest days of our lives."

We all went to the Easter service in the old parish church above the village. Everyone in Brusje was there that day, and when they sang the Easter hymns with their magnificent Dalmatian voices I was transported into a world without weaklings, a place where life is tough and the choices are few, but a better world, perhaps, despite the hardships.

*   *   *   *   *   *

We had been invited to lunch in Hvar Town by Jakov and Matica's eldest daughter, Katica, and her husband, Nikola, who own a charming villa overlooking the sea. We drove our friends down to the town after church, and sat on a bench under some palm trees looking out towards the Pakleni Isles and distant Vis.

Nikola is a heart specialist who works in a hospital in Zagreb, and the first time we met him was on the occasion of his marriage to Katica in the early 1970s. Following the old tradition, he and his family had climbed up the mountain road to Brusje bearing an apple stuffed with gold pieces on the morning of the wedding. They knocked loudly on Jakov's door, and when it had been opened a crack a gruff voice inside asked: "Who's there?"

Nikola's father announced that he had come to buy a woman. The bride was nowhere to be seen, but various old crones were brought forward, one after another, and each time Nikola's father shook his head vigorously. A vision in white suddenly appeared at the top of the stairs, and the bridegroom and his family roared "That's the woman we want to buy!"

And Katica came slowly down the stairs ...

The ground floor of their villa in Hvar had a small kitchen on an upper level leading down into a beautiful white living-room with a polished wood floor. There were a few pictures and pieces of sculpture, a round table and some comfortable chairs and the shadows of the palm leaves dancing on the sunlit walls and ceiling. We sat around the table, Jakov, Matica, Maja – their fourteen-year-old granddaughter – Dick and I, while Niko poured out the finest wine of Hvar and Katica produced some marvellous dishes – specialities for Easter, we were told – from her kitchen. It was a very happy party and a day we shall long remember; and Maja, who was learning English at school, proved to be an intelligent and delightful member of the family. But this was another world from the mountain village of Brusje – a sophisticated charming world that was far removed from the hours of toil on a scorching mountainside, the uncertain harvests of rosemary and lavender oil and the donkey and the mule to bring the fruits of their labour into market, if any market still existed.

Later that day we sat in Jakov and Matica's kitchen drinking a last glass of *Prošek* before returning to Jelsa.

"You must pack your bags and return here immediately," Matica urged. "We cannot permit you to stay a moment longer in that miserable hotel."

We had foreseen this conversation, but knew only too well that the intolerable strain of feeding guests was something we would never have wished to impose on our friends at that time.

"It is not possible, as much as we would love to spend all our time with you," I replied. "Because we paid for our room at the Hotel Mina before leaving England."

This, I surmised, would be an argument Matica would find hard to resist, as one never threw money down the drain in her native Dalmatia any more than one did in my native Yorkshire! Seeing a shadow of doubt in her eyes, we pressed home our advantage.

"Tomorrow we will call for you before midday," Dick declared; "as I have already arranged with Niko that you will all be our guests at the Hotel Slavija."

Jakov looked rather belligerent, as if his pride was being hurt; but Matica's eyes lit up with pleasure and she announced that she would be able to wear her new shoes again and also, perhaps, the blouse we had brought her from England.

$$* \quad * \quad * \quad * \quad * \quad *$$

Easter Monday was another perfect day. We lay on the smooth-faced rocks under the pine trees after breakfast, gazing at the cornflower-blue sky, the dazzle of silver and gold where the sunbeams came slanting through the upper branches and the little red lighthouse on the end of the point. A fisherman stood on a rock nearby, casting his line with hope, and a blackbird sang like a bird in love among the thick foliage of a eucalyptus tree.

"It's like a page from one of my favourite books, 'Illyrian Spring' by

The Cathedral Square in Hvar Town.

Jakov, Matica and me leaving Brusje.

Anne Bridge," I told Dick, as we dusted the pine needles off each others' backs and tried to make ourselves appear respectable for the lunch-party.

We picked up Jakov and Matica, looking intensely smart, half an hour later. Dick and Jakov sang lustily all the way down the twisting mountain road, and they had just reached a crescendo on the outskirts of Hvar Town when Dick, who was conducting the duet with his left hand, took the wrong turning down a one way street where we came face to face with a police car driving the other way. The policeman leapt out of his vehicle and advanced on the Citroen with his purple cheeks puffed out with rage.

Dick reluctantly wound down his window and the man began to roar at him in ear-piercing Croatian. Matica, simultaneously, slipped out of the passenger seat and strode round the bonnet to confront the law. I have no idea what she said – only that she resembled an Amazon on the warpath in ancient times. The policeman blanched and seemed to shrivel inside his uniform as he offered his profound apologies, and invited Dick to follow him to an excellent parking-place near the main square.

We had arrived early so we strolled around the centre of Hvar which radiated warmth and beauty, whichever way you looked. High up on the crests of the surrounding hills stand the two forts, the Spanish one built in the thirteenth century and strengthened by the Venetians three centuries later, and Fort Napoleon, built by the French during their brief occupation of the island from 1806 till 1813. Two immense crenellated walls, with watch-towers at each angle, descend the hillside on either hand, clasping the old town between their feet when they reach the neighbourhood of the sea.

The main square is a glorious place paved with slabs of creamy-white stone; and it has a Venetian well reposing in the middle of it which is still in use. The Cathedral of Sveti Stefan, with its tall rectangular campanile, stands sentinel at the far end; then there is the Paladini Palace on one side and the famous Venetian Arsenal on the other and, just above it, the oldest theatre in the former Jugoslavia, built in 1612. The green mountain slopes, the honey-coloured buildings, the palm trees along the waterfront and the blue waters of the harbour completed that dreamlike scene, which looked more beautiful than we remembered without the usual crush of arrogant, half-naked tourists.

Katica, Niko and Maja met us by the small boat harbour, and they had reserved a table in the restaurant of the Hotel Slavija near the ferry-boat quay. Jakov tugged unhappily at his tight collar and Dick exchanged glances of sympathy with him across the table. The menu, however, was clearly a source of intense interest to all our guests and, after long consultations with the waiter, a rare fish was chosen by most of the family, apart from Maja and I, who preferred the idea of spaghetti.

"What do you think of President Tudjman?" Dick asked Niko, while we waited for the main course.

He pondered for some minutes and seemed to be searching for the right words to express his thoughts. "He started the war as a general without fame, and now he and his wife have acquired various factories, at home and abroad, and they will soon be millionaires, you understand? But he, who has never done anything great for his country, wishes now to destroy our history and the memory of the brave men who fought for our freedom fifty years ago. I had a cousin, a hero in 1944, who was shot by the Gestapo. After the war they erected a statue of him in Zagreb, but already it has been removed.

"I think that we shall have much trouble in Croatia before long; Istria and Dalmatia would like to break away and become separate states, and Tudjman's government acts in ways that preclude all chances of peace in Krajina. His army is not strong enough to thrust out the Serbs, and the UN presence there separates the hostile ethnic communities for so long, that they will never have the chance nor the desire to live peacefully together again.

"Also there is the question of the refugees. There are 3.9 million since the war started, and more than 40,000 children have lost all contact with their parents. We, in Croatia, have more than 600,000 and we cannot afford to support them. Always we need more help from the outside world than they can give us. And, in the meantime, our poor refugees have not enough to eat and no future. You are lucky to live in a country without such *problemas*!"

The fish course arrived and deep concentration descended on our table, apart from one end where Maja and I were chatting happily about London life.

"Please describe for me all your favourite things in London," she pleaded, "because I have a great desire to go there one day, as soon as I am old enough."

After lunch we stood on the waterfront watching a fisherman mending his nets, while a small dog sat on the bows of a neighbouring boat, as motionless as the samson-post against which he leant. All too soon it was time for Katica and Maja to catch a bus for their long and dangerous journey back to Zagreb. Katica worked in a travel office there and Maja was due back at school next day.

We drove Jakov and Matica home, and promised to call and see them for a farewell drink on our way back to Hvar to catch the ferry next day.

*   *   *   *   *   *

It was so sad, that last visit to Brusje. We had been urged to leave the Hotel Mina in good time as they were going to close the whole place immediately after our departure.

"Good luck in June," we wished the young woman in Reception, as we trundled our remaining eight suitcases out to the car.

She smiled uncertainly and called out *"Do vidjenja i sretan put!"* across the vast marble acres of the entrance hall.

We found Jakov and Matica waiting for us in their home, with a row of parcels lined up on the kitchen table. There were bottles of *raki* and *Prošek* and wine of Hvar, more bottles of virgin olive oil, lavender and rosemary oil, a huge pot of honey, a loaf of freshly baked bread, a cake and some music tapes of Jakov's nephew singing the songs of Hvar Island.

Matica made coffee and pressed us to eat their special Easter cakes, and she confided to me that Niko, who was remaining in Hvar two days longer, would be coming to dine with them that evening to share the roast of beef!

We sat there for a few minutes longer, all on the verge of tears. Then a neighbour looked in to borrow some flour, and we hugged our old friends and drove away down the mountain road without looking back.

The ferry to Rijeka was called SLAVIJA, a big vessel with five decks above the waterline which towered over the crowded waterfront and the shops and kiosks behind it. Niko came to see us off; he stood under a palm tree waving to us long after the ship had let go her mooring lines and was moving rapidly astern towards the open sea.

Chapter 19 - Our New Friends

The Splitska Vrata from the terrace of olive trees.

The SLAVIJA took us back through the Splitska Vrata, past all those nostalgic memories of favourite coves where we had anchored in the past, then across the Brački Kanal to Split. The Morris family – Paul, Sheila and Chris – were waiting for us on the quayside, and they came aboard for coffee and a chat while the ship was loading her cargo for Zadar and Rijeka. Half an hour later we were ready to sail. No messing about nor last minute delays on the Jadrolinija ferries: they came and left on the dot, and it was hard luck for any visitors who were trapped aboard when the gangway had just been raised!

We hung over the ship's quarter waving goodbye to our friends while the sun set dramatically behind the little chapel on the summit of a hill on Veli Drvenik Island. I began to shiver as we groped our way down the dark companionway to the dining-saloon.

"They don't show a blaze of lights on these ships," Paul had warned us; "in case some Serb gunners up in the mountains feel like doing a bit of target practice, see what I mean?"

We had a lovely cabin – Number 83 – on the port side of the bows, two decks above the waterline. Dick, once again, generously offered me the bunk beside the porthole, and there I knelt for several hours with my nose pressed against the glass as the long thin Kornati Islands slid silently by outside. An occasional lighthouse flashed from a headland or an isolated rock, otherwise there was nothing but the steady thump-thump of the engines and the swish of our bow-wave as we sped across the calm night sea.

I began to feel drowsy, and was just about to get into my bunk when the engine noises changed; we had slowed right down and were clearly waiting for something ...? I could see two lights through the porthole: a powerful white one from the islet of Ošljak, and a green one that flashed every two seconds from Preko, a port on Ugljan Island.

We stayed where we were, suspended in space it almost seemed, for at least twenty minutes; then the Captain must have rung full speed ahead on his bridge telegraph, because the SLAVIJA leapt forward and I nearly fell off my bunk. A few minutes later she came alongside an outer mole in Zadar harbour, the big doors on her quarter slid open to allow a few cars to escape and, immediately, several others drove aboard. The doors ground together, the seamen hauled in their lines, fore and aft, and the engines were engaged in full speed astern.

The last I saw of Zadar was a big white-flashing lighthouse on the end of a jetty. No shells that night, and we were soon speeding north again, through the sleeping archipelago.

*   *   *   *   *   *

We woke up in a different world. The sky was covered with heavy grey clouds and the mountains bordering the coast looked small and insignificant. I rubbed my eyes to see if I was dreaming, but no; there lay the great port of Rijeka with its tall blocks of flats, off-white and grey, like the sky above them; the sprawl of houses climbing up the hillside, whichever way you looked; the long harbour wall with ship's funnels and masts rising above it, and more ships – tankers and merchantmen – anchored outside. Then I looked north towards the far horizon and saw some snow-capped peaks floating among the heavy grey clouds.

It was seven o'clock in the morning when the SLAVIJA came alongside the ferry-boat terminal in Rijeka. No time for breakfast – already the stewards were bustling around in the cabins, getting them ready for the southbound passengers. We seized our bags and ran down to the car-deck where the bo'sun was issuing governessy instructions to the drivers. A few minutes later we were out in the main street in Rijeka, dodging trams and white UN vehicles as we headed north-west towards the coastal road that runs round the edge of the Kvarner Gulf.

Opatija was only seven miles away, the town where Mick Gelsthorpe and his tribe had stayed nearly two years ago while they searched for refugees to bring back to England. Built around a fifteenth century convent, it first emerged from being little more than a sleepy seaside village in 1879, when a Croatian doctor persuaded a Viennese colleague to encourage his patients to visit Opatija for their health.

"It has high mountains, sub-tropical vegetation, luxuriant gardens, golden beaches, and a perfect climate," he urged; "and they will be able to sunbathe there for at least five months each year."

About the same time Anne-Marie of Savoy, the Austro-Hungarian Empress, brought a bathing-machine to this miraculous village and made salt-water bathing respectable for the upper classes. Three years later, the company which had brought the railway line to Rijeka, bought the land round some holiday villas in Opatija and built the first big hotel. A medical congress was convened there in 1885, and it proclaimed the place a health resort.

The town, since then, has gradually grown into one enormous hotel, pension, private apartment, chalet, yacht harbour and beach-hut complex which has provided holiday accommodation for thousands of German, Austrian, Hungarian, Italian and other invalids and tourists, for more than a century. But now, of course, the greater part of the town is used to house countless refugees from other parts of Croatia and from Bosnia.

We drove into town and soon found ourselves in the main street which was lined with palm trees. Handsome buildings, reminiscent of the Austro-Hungarian Empire, rose up on either side of us; also there were bustling tourist shops and small markets, a blockage of impatient cars and women in black clothes sitting on a low wall along the sea front, displaying their beautiful crochet-work. I noticed that many of the tall buildings had lines of multi-coloured washing pegged out along their very ornate balconies.

We came to the Hotel Admiral at last, a hideous modern pile where we were booked to stay for the next three nights. But the press of traffic was so intense and the parking spaces so rare, that we had to circle the town twice on a complicated one-way system before we could stop anywhere near our target. There were only eight important suitcases left in the Citroen when we found our way to the reception desk and confirmed our

Opatija from our balcony at the Hotel Admiral.

booking. A boy ran out with a trolley to fetch our luggage and the head of Reception was quite charming, but the hotel looked rather grand and intimidating to a pair of scruffy travellers with far too many suitcases.

It was breakfast-time in Opatija and, unlike the Hotel Mina at Jelsa, the Admiral's dining-room was nearly full. Plump German and Hungarian matrons jockeyed for position round a big central table laden with cereals, fruit juice, egg dishes, ham, cheese, toast and rolls, while a number of attractive waitresses poured coffee or tea into their cups. It all seemed so far removed from the war in Bosnia and Krajina, and the starving families in the south, that we sat at our table gazing around us with astonishment. Shortly after our arrival a table near us filled up with a dozen or more young Danish soldiers, on leave from some UN base in Croatia. Their appetites were even healthier than the Germans, but they treated the staff with more appreciation.

We had promised to visit Anica at Lovran on our first day, so we left the Hotel Admiral feeling rather sick and walked to the shopping centre to buy a few extra presents: some cheese and wine, and a special thread used by the women for their crochet-work.

The road to Lovran followed the coast beside the Kvarner Gulf, and there were woods filled with chestnut trees and laurels climbing up the hills on our right-hand side. Lovran, which means 'laurel', is a very old town founded by the Slavs in the sixth century, but it was not until the late nineteenth century that it became a popular resort filled with hotels and pensions.

Ten minutes after leaving Opatija we drove into the pretty little town – so short had been our journey, in fact, that we were taken quite by surprise when a shabby building called the Villa Atlanta loomed ahead of us...

"Look!" I grabbed Dick's arm, causing him to swerve. "There's Anica standing up there on the steps!"

She was wearing a red jersey and pale blue jeans, and there were tears in all our eyes when we hugged and kissed each other on the steps of the Villa Atlanta.

"Come inside at once," she ordered us; "I have the coffee almost ready in case you arrived, and my sister and her little girl is here with me – you know, my sister from Slovenia?"

She led the way along a passage filled with curious eyes – other refugees who had left their doors ajar to catch a glimpse of these rare visitors from who knew where. We turned a corner and were ushered into the Hržić family's home.

My first impression was of a brownish-beige coloured room with heavy net curtains covering the windows, and beds ... lots of beds, whichever

In Anica's room at the Villa Atlanta at Lovran. Anica with her sister, Mira, and her daughter.

Zvonko, Ante, Anica and Josip at Lovran.

way you looked. Of course there were other things like a small striped sofa and matching armchair, and a polished wood table partially covered with one of Anica's embroidered table-cloths on which stood plates laden with freshly-baked white bread, sausage-meat, cheese, sweet-meats and some splendid white cakes the shape of starboard-hand buoys.

"What a wonderful feast you have prepared for us!" Dick told Anica who was brewing the coffee, while I conversed with her sister, Mira. She told me that she had come to Lovran to be near her mother-in-law who was dying in hospital in Rijeka.

Mira's little girl had a very sweet face below a severely cut fringe, with eyes as big and round as golf balls which were fixed unblinkingly on the plateful of cakes. Her mother looked emaciated, very pale and rather ill; and when I looked at Anica again I noticed that she had lost a lot of weight and looked hardly any better than her sister. But she smiled happily as she helped me unpack the suitcases we had brought, and received presents from Bill and Amelia, and Ted and Eileen that we had concealed among the clothes.

Anica's best china teacups and plates were on the table that day, and she had the coffee-pot poised over my cup to refill it while she implored us; "Eat more, my dear friends; you eat like small birds and there is much to ..."

The door flew open at that moment to admit a tall and very angry man. He stomped into the middle of the room and pointed an accusing finger at Dick.

"What are you doing in this place?" he roared; "when I have prepared lunch for you and have been waiting to receive you in my home for at least one hour?"

He swung round slowly and allowed his ferocious gaze to rest on Anica, then on me; and suddenly I realized that we were looking at Zvonko, Marica's husband, but a different Zvonko to the charming courteous man we had met in England. Dick, who is the best person I know at pouring oil on turbulent seas, stood up and embraced Zvonko in the true Croatian style, then declared (quite truthfully) that he had no idea we had been invited to lunch as we had only just arrived from Dalmatia on the overnight ferry.

"We drove to Lovran looking for your hotel," he explained tactfully, "but the first person we saw was Anica standing outside the Villa Atlanta, so we changed our plans and had decided to visit you a little later in the day."

Zvonko appeared mollified with Dick's explanation and, at that moment, the door swung open again and a young man walked into the room and shook us both by the hand.

"I am Ante Marić, Marica's brother," he informed us; "and I come to greet you and to ask news of my sister?"

The door opened for the third time to admit Josip, just home from morning school. Kisses were exchanged and I noticed that the beds were filling up, with numerous pairs of hungry eyes riveted to the spread on Anica's coffee-table. But Zvonko had other plans and was not to be diverted.

"You will all follow me to the Hotel Lovran," he commanded; "and there we will eat lunch together."

Anica's sister and her daughter refused, because it was time for her to return to the hospital to sit with her mother-in-law. But an older man, who was a friend of Zvonko's, joined us in the garden, and we were a party of seven who sat down to lunch in the dining-room of the Hotel Lovran. Clearly a great deal of trouble had been taken over the menu and the style of our entertainment, and Dick and I were deeply touched by the whole business when we recalled the scarcity of food and the poor quality normally allotted to the refugee hostels. Zvonko was an excellent host, and the two waiters joined in with the lively conversation and the toasts which were being proposed all round the table.

I had just raised a fork laden with savoury mincemeat to my mouth, when a flash of light drew my eyes towards a young man squatting behind a tripod, his camera focussed on our table like a machine-gun ready for action. He flashed away happily, fifteen or twenty times, and I whispered to Dick; "They must have sent for the local Press to record our visit!"

Zvonko's lunch-party at the Hotel Lovran: Zvonko, Ante, Dick, Josip, Anica and a friend of Zvonko's.

Zvonko giving us presents in his room. Anica, me and Dick on the bed.

Anica asked me what plans we had made for our brief stay in Opatija. I told her that we were going to Kostrena next day to visit Janja and Filip and their family, and asked if she would like to come with us. She had just opened her mouth to say "Yes", when Josip intervened.

"You must not go, Mama," he told her quite firmly, "or you will spoil the occasion for Janja who, doubtless, has made her own special preparations."

Anica looked very disappointed, but was reluctantly prepared to obey her twelve-year-old son.

"We wish to ask you, Josip, Marjan, Antonija and your sister and her little girl to have dinner with us at the Hotel Admiral on our last evening?" I proposed, whereupon Anica's crestfallen face resembled a rain-cloud pierced by brilliant sunbeams.

Zvonko rose to his feet as soon as we had finished our lunch and announced; "I will now show you our garden and the sea front at Lovran; then we will return to MY room."

He placed great emphasis on the "MY", to make sure of quashing any plans we might have nurtured of slipping back to Anica's room instead!

The Hotel Lovran was a sad-looking building with a beige exterior and a large glass porch where we posed once again for a number of group photographs. An old lady dressed in the Slavonian national costume joined the party on this occasion. The garden was filled with an exotic mixture of overgrown trees and shrubs: pines, laurels, magnolias, Judas trees, cypresses, fig trees, coconut trees and the spiky yucca plant, which smelt of butterscotch.

We soon reached the waterfront and strolled along it towards a small harbour crammed with boats, and the Kvarner Restaurant built on a promontory above it. Beyond that we could see a jetty ending in a lighthouse, and a solitary fisherman sitting in an old wooden dinghy, fishing for dear life off the point. Away to the south the mountains of Cres and Krk rose mysteriously out of a sea of opals. I glanced inland as we turned to follow Zvonko back to his home, and saw the square tower of a church with a spire emerging from the top of it, the whole building painted primrose-yellow with bands of white outlining the tower.

A few minutes later he ushered us into a small single room on the second floor of the Hotel Lovran, after passing a row of half-opened doors filled with dark yearning eyes fixed on us like searchlights. Dick had fetched a suitcase from the car which was packed with presents from Zvonko's family and us, and we were offered seats on the bed which occupied one third of the room while he received the parcels with some reluctance, and immediately squirrelled them away under the bed. I felt rather disappointed that he would not look at the recent photographs of his wife and children we had taken especially on his account, nor a copy of Ivana's drawing which was in the exhibition at the Imperial War Museum at that time.

"I keep all the photographs of my family in this box," he told us, pulling a cardboard shoe-box from under the bed. "You must understand that I cannot pin them up on the walls like other people do in this place, because it would make me feel too sad."

He had a better view than the one from Anica's room, as I could see a red-tiled roof and some green foliage behind it; but the main trouble was that he had nothing to do all day and no money to spend out in the town. The women suffered less in that way as there were the children to look after, a small amount of housework, plenty of washing to do and their beautiful *ručni rad* – the crochet-work and embroidery they hoped to sell to the tourists. But the men stood no chance of finding a job locally; and unless they could turn their hands to other skills like carving or model-making, there were hours and hours of blank nothingness to be lived through each day, with very little to hope for in the future.

Zvonko's bed rapidly filled up: there was Anica, Ante, Josip and us, as well as one or two friends from further along the corridor and a young man from Ilok, Zvonko's home town near Vukovar, who turned out to be the photographer. He continued flashing away at the group established on the bed all the time we were there.

Dick and I came under attack from Zvonko after our arrival. Luckily, perhaps, we could not understand very much of what he was saying as he spoke very rapidly in a face to face close encounter situation; and there was no means of escape which made me feel nervous and unable to translate reliably for Dick. Anica helped me to gather the gist of his complaints which all concerned his family in England.

"Did we know about this regrettable boyfriend of Marijana's, because he would never permit his daughter to marry a foreigner who could not even speak a word of Croatian? Why had Ivana been allowed to become entangled with that crazy artists' nonsense in London. And what was the meaning of Damir telling him on the telephone about some trophy he had won at *tae-kwondo*? Surely this was a dangerous pastime, only suitable for young thugs? Why was Marica not looking after his children with more firmness and discretion?"

"Are you telling us that you want your family to come back to Lovran now?" I asked him, half-mesmerized by that eyeball to eyeball business.

"No, I do not mean to say that. Of course I am very grateful for all the good things they have received in England which they could not have had if they had remained here. But as soon as I can make a new home for them in Croatia, I want them back."

You'll be lucky, I thought to myself; but I smiled serenely and said, "I can well understand your feelings, and I'm sure they must feel the same."

Dick looked at his watch and Zvonko, who noticed the gesture, brought the lecturing part of his programme to a sudden conclusion.

"I have a few little parcels here which are for you and your family," he declared, his face illuminated like an Oriental sunrise. Zvonko the courtier was back on the stage.

The boy from Ilok, who had joined us on the bed to show us his album of the historic buildings in his home town before the Serbs destroyed them, sprang into action at that point. He crouched in the doorway of the room with his camera on its tripod, ready to fire. Many weeks later we received a packet of photographs from Zvonko; and suddenly we realized that he must have organized the whole business before our arrival, to have a complete pictorial record of our visit to the Hotel Lovran!

We were not allowed to open our parcels right away, but Dick invited Zvonko to dinner at the Hotel Admiral in two days' time, and promised to collect him and Anica and her family at seven o'clock that evening. Ante had come on the bus from Opatija to meet us, so we offered him a lift back there in the Citroen.

Ante's wife was also called Anica, and when we drew up outside the Hotel Zagreb he insisted that we should come inside and meet her. Their home was in a shabby-looking pile built of beige-coloured concrete, the balconies festooned with washing; and the Marić family's one room was almost entirely occupied by a double-bed and a cot. Anica and Baby Marija were asleep on the bed when we arrived, and they awoke with some astonishment to find a pair of total strangers peering at them.

Anica Marić, Marija and Ante Marić in their room at the Hotel Zagreb.

The wallpaper had perpendicular stripes on a pinkish background with olive-green leaves included in the pattern, and a selection of soft toys occupied the adjacent pillow. Baby Marija was dressed in turquoise-blue velveteen knickerbockers with red buttons down the middle and red bands round her legs. She had large brown eyes and a lovely smile that seldom left her face, while her proud parents showed us many photographs of their home near Ilok, before the Serbs seized it, of their families in Hercegovina, their wedding and the first days of Marija's life.

I was struck by the aura of happiness which filled that humble home, like an Arctic tundra that has suddenly burst into a carpet of beautiful flowers. Baby Marija was born in the refugee hostel so she knew no other life with which to compare it; and, judging by the pride and devotion that surrounded her, we knew that her guardian angel was not far away in that twilight world of the ethnically cleansed people of Croatia.

Later that evening we sat down to dinner in the bustling dining-room of the Hotel Admiral. The Danish UN soldiers had clearly been drinking for much of the day, but the waitresses were well-practised in swinging their hips to one side to avoid pairs of hands like lobster's claws trying to pinch their bottoms. Other tables were occupied by middle-aged couples from

Vienna and Munich, the men with important stomachs and gimlet eyes focussed with envy on the lusty Danes, while their partners stared severely into space.

"Do you think we could book a large table for ten people on Friday evening?" Dick asked the head-waiter when we had finished our meal. "We have invited eight guests, you see, but one of them is only a baby."

"*Nije problema!*" the man grinned cheerfully. "I put you at that long table over there, as you will have more peacefulness to converse with your friends in that part of the room; also we have a baby-chair that I will fix for you."

Dick thanked him for his kindness as we stepped into the lift.

"I wonder if he'd smile so sweetly if he knew they were refugees?" I mused as the doors began to close. "I do hope it will be all right when Friday evening comes, and the staff and visitors in this rather grand place won't be horrid to our friends."

"Don't see why they should be," Dick replied. "After all, some of them may be refugees themselves."

*   *   *   *   *   *

The road to Kostrena was broad and shining, with long curves and switchbacks that took us across the flanks of the mountains guarding the head of the Kvarner Gulf. We rose rapidly out of Opatija, past shabby villas lounging in overgrown gardens; then up on to a rocky plateau where the snow-capped summits of the Slovenian mountains touched the pale blue sky away to the north.

A few miles further on the city of Rijeka unfolded below us: smoking factory chimneys, tall grey and white tenements, the Petroleum Harbour, broad jetties jutting out from the shore, immense harbour walls, several lighthouses and the masts, derricks and funnels of a number of merchant ships. I could see the soft pink and mauve contours of Krk and Cres Islands over on the far horizon, and even a hint of the Lovran coastline.

The road suddenly dipped down towards the valley of the River Rječina, from which the city took its name. Before the Second World War it formed the frontier between Italy and Jugoslavia. We crossed a bridge over the river, and just above us I could see the hamlet of Trsar clinging to the suburbs of Rijeka like a precious jewel attached to the rump of an elephant. In the middle of a grove of cypresses and eucalyptus trees stands a little Franciscan convent, and nearby was once the home of a widow called Agatha in whose garden the Ark of the Covenant was set down by the angels from Nazareth in 1291. It rested there for three and a half years, performing miraculous cures for the sick people who came to visit it, before it suddenly took off one stormy night in December to continue on its journey to Loretto in Italy.   .

We climbed skywards again, with the eastern suburbs of the city rising up to meet the road until it took a sharp bend inland and made a U-turn round an inlet filled with one enormous ship, some tall cranes and large sheds.

"What an amazing secret cove in which to hide a shipbuilding yard!" I exclaimed, but Dick was too busy negotiating the hairpin bend at the head of the inlet to comment. And when we reached the next corner, a signpost announced "Kostrena – 2 km."

Kostrena was a place without a heart – no central square with a church around which the village had grown up. In fact the name covered part of a peninsula, with a spine of hills running down the centre and a cluster of lighthouses guarding the south-eastern extremity.

About two minutes later we saw a sign pointing to the Hotel Lucija, and turned sharp right into a tree-lined drive which led us to the parking space outside a small hotel. It looked rather nice and cosy, and it appeared that there were visitors staying there as a number of German cars were parked outside, and not a single washed garment could be seen fluttering from any of the balconies.

"That's strange," Dick observed. "Are you sure you've got the right address?"

"Yes, it's definitely the Hotel Lucija, Kostrena," I confirmed. "Let's go inside and see if we can find them."

The woman in Reception raised her eyes towards the ceiling when I asked for the Franjković family, and told us they lived in the other building. You walked through the garden towards the sea and it stood among the trees, just above the beach.

"I will phone them to announce your arrival," she said; "and if you wait outside, they will come here to fetch you."

"I expect she wants to keep us out of sight of the paying guests," I laughed to Dick as we strolled back to the car and disembarked our last two suitcases. "I suppose we do look a bit scruffy after all our journeys!"

Janja came running round the corner at that moment – a very smart Janja wearing a green and mauve striped jersey, a black skirt and sheer silk stockings. Mind you, I did not notice any of those details at the time as she enclosed us each in a bear's hug that took our breath away and implanted four kisses – two per cheek – on each of our faces. Suddenly I felt really glad that we had come. Only rarely does a welcome seem so heartfelt, and it was good to know that the saga of the fifteen suitcases would end on such a happy note.

Janja ushered us into a smallish room filled, no surprise this time, with beds. But the walls were white and a glass door led out on to a small balcony from which you could see pine trees and tamarisks, and the rocky foreshore with a blue blue sea beyond.

"How lovely!" I exclaimed; "This is the best home we have seen."

"But you have not seen all," she announced, pulling me across the corridor. "You see we are so lucky because we have TWO rooms for our family; this is where Filip and I sleep."

She led me into a supremely tidy little room which also had plain white walls and a painting of an Adriatic fishing-boat above the bed; and, luxury of luxuries, a small cooker and basin for washing up in the far corner.

"Is it not *supair?*" she smiled proudly as we returned to the other room where Dick was making the acquaintance of two elderly ladies dressed in black, and a young woman whose face looked vaguely familiar.

"This is Filip's mother," Janja introduced us to the oldest lady first. "And this is Katica's mother who has come down from the mountains in Krajina specially to meet you; and her sister from Senj, further along the coast."

Ruža Matasić, Katica's mother, was exactly like her daughter in England – the same bright blue eyes and gentle face, with a slightly quizzical expression that could suddenly break into a radiant smile, like a rainbow after a heavy downpour. I felt that we were already old friends because it was she who had provided that historic bottle of *šljivovic* which Katica shared with all of us on her first night at Thoresby. And I had corresponded with her since then, and enjoyed wearing the pair of slippers she made for me last Christmas.

There was much embracing and implanting of kisses on both cheeks, then Janja invited us all to be seated while she made the coffee.

Ruža Matasić and her daughter from Senj.

"Filip and the children will soon be home," she told us, aware of the five pairs of eyes trained upon the plates of chicken slices, ham and sausage-meat laid out on the table; "then we will eat."

Janja

We had planned to take the whole family out to lunch in the best restaurant we could find in Kostrena, as we knew that the journey to Opatija would be too long and expensive for them to make on Friday evening. And the two families, in Lovran and Kostrena, were not perhaps the closest of friends. Dick tried to explain our plan to Janja and Ruža with me acting as interpreter; but the two women looked rather vague and Janja said they must wait for Dragana, who would not return from school till after two o'clock. And had we not observed the lovely chicken and home-cured ham that Ruža had brought with her from Ličko Lešće, her home in Krajina? Filip's mother nodded her head sagely, and Katica's sister explained that she herself had baked the loaf of bread only yesterday.

Dick and I glanced at each other with question marks in our eyes, foreseeing a *problema* arising if we became too insistent.

"Let me show you what Katica and Malcolm and Cynthia have sent you," I said to Janja, while I began to unpack the last suitcases and hand out the various packages we had brought from England.

There was much clucking and sighing, and many *krasnos* and *odličnos* resounded across the room as Janja and Ruža drew out pullovers, blouses, knitting-wool, medicines, soap, face-cream, material for making clothes, foodstuffs, etc, and clasped them to their bosoms with eyes raised to the ceiling. Luckily one of the suitcases had been filled with presents for Ruža – just in case we did have the chance to meet her. She lived in a remote mountain village very near the front line, and her house and garden had sometimes been damaged by shells from the Serb guns exploding nearby, even though the UN Peace-Keepers were supposed to preserve the peace in Krajina.

"You get used to it," she told us with a smile. "And in the end you hardly notice these horrors that come raining down out of the sky. But some of my neighbours have not been so fortunate, I can assure you."

Her daughter put a protective arm around her mother's shoulders and said it was better where she and her husband lived by the sea in Senj; but she had many anxious moments when the shelling started again up above in Krajina.

Filip came home some while later, then Dragan returned from morning school. We were coaxed to eat and drink by all our hosts, and as soon as I had finished a slice of bread and ham, I was plied with a chicken leg or some other rare treat brought by one of Janja's guests. Dragan ate with gusto, and Filip produced a bottle of *Prošek* with which we drank a number of toasts – to absent friends, the end of the war and a future of peace and happiness.

It was two o'clock by that time, and Dick and I were beginning to wonder how on earth we could extricate our friends and take them out to lunch? Filip looked very solemn and down-hearted.

"Look at my hands!" he said to Dick; "they are becoming soft and useless from sitting here all day doing nothing. You say we have nice rooms and a pretty view of the sea, but when all this comes to an end I

Dragana   *Dragan*

hope I never see the sea again, as long as I live! I go fishing with Dragan when he's not at school and we have enough to eat. But this is no life for a man who wishes to work for the good of his family. It's like sitting in a dark hole with no glimmer of light at the end of the tunnel."

He slumped in his chair and the women looked at him sadly. For them, the struggle to keep a neat and shining home and chase the devils of despair from their two cramped rooms was just as hard an ordeal, I suspected.

Dragana was the last one to come home. "It takes me one hour each way on the bus to my school in Opatija," she told us. "It is very hard work there and I have to learn four languages – English, German, Italian and Croatian. And sometimes it is dangerous to stay late at school because of all the drunken soldiers who come to Opatija to make pleasure – those UN pigs, you understand?"

We were slowly beginning to understand that many of our previous concepts about life in Croatia were rather out of date. Dragana, meanwhile, helped herself ravenously to the unaccustomed feast.

Now that we had an English speaker with us, Dick appealed to the girl; "Please tell your parents that we wish to take you all out to lunch at the best restaurant you can recommend in Kostrena. And shouldn't we soon be going there now that you are back home?"

Dragana translated, and there was a pregnant pause. Dragan rolled his eyeballs so that there were only two segments of white visible, then Ruža looked at her watch and declared that her bus back to Ličko Lešće would be leaving in half an hour's time, and she had brought with her a few presents for us and Katica and the children that she hoped we wouldn't mind taking back to England with us. She pulled out from under her chair an immense package wrapped in brown paper which she handed to Dick, who staggered like a drunken man under its weight. Everyone began to laugh, and I had a sudden vision of this little oldish lady in black making her long and dangerous journey down from the mountains, carrying her package with a straight back and head held high.

Janja stood up and announced; "We will all go to the Bistro San Lucija, just up the road. It is very close to the bus-stop and Ruža will have time to come with us. But, before we go, Filip and I also have some presents for you to take to England."

She opened a cupboard and drew out a number of parcels labelled "Katica" and *"Molkom i Sintija"* and, finally, a pair of magnificent shell ornaments – one a 3-masted sailing-ship and the other a pair of seagulls perched on big shells – for Dick and me.

"What a lovely surprise!" I exclaimed; "but you shouldn't have got us presents too, after this wonderful feast and everything else." I could feel hot tears rolling down my cheeks, but luckily everyone was busy collecting their coats and bags to go out, so they did not notice me.

We strolled through the gardens of the Hotel Lucija with our friends, put our parcels in the car, then climbed up a short hill to the Bistro San Lucija which stood on a plateau above the main road. It very soon transpired that the bistro only served coffee, Coca-Cola and ice-creams, so Dick and I were defeated in our purpose after all. I noticed Janja and her mother-in-law exchanging happy glances of complicity, and everyone relaxed as we sat down and ordered a selection of the three items on the menu.

Our few hours in Kostrena had passed so quickly, and already the last photographs were being taken and messages composed for us to take back to friends in England. Dragana asked for a copy of Natali's essay with which she had won first prize in school; also many photographs of the Jerbić family and Thoresby.

"Life is so hard for us here," she said rather bitterly, confident that her mother could not understand much English. "Sometimes I wish we'd never left England. There is no room to move in our place. As you saw, it is nothing but beds, beds ... And the Croatian people in this part do not want us. Already they have too many refugees, they say, and more coming each day from Bosnia. How will it all end?"

Ruža and her daughter were standing up and collecting their bags together, as the bus was due in a few minutes' time. Dick went inside the café to pay the bill, then we were all standing out on the road saying "*Do vidjenja*" and "*sretan put*", and trying to smile instead of bursting into tears.

We drove away down the main highway, past the shipbuilding yard and the sprawling city of Rijeka. I felt glad that we had seen all our friends and safely delivered the contents of our suitcases; but sad that tomorrow would be our last day in Croatia.

"Josip was quite right," Dick broke in on my thoughts. "I think it would have spoilt Janja's day if we'd brought Anica along with us. The headmaster at his school in Mansfield had a very high opinion of his intelligence."

Later that evening, back in our room at the Hotel Admiral, Dick surveyed our luggage and sighed. "Do you realize that we've got almost as much to take back to England as we started with? There are all the presents from Brač and Hvar, as well as the latest parcels from Anica, Zvonko, Janja and Katica's mother and sister. But I'm not prepared to cross five frontiers without knowing what's inside that huge package from Ruža. Supposing there are drugs or something like that concealed inside it?"

"Well, we'd better have a look," I agreed; "although I think it's extremely unlikely that she would want to use us to smuggle her drugs into England."

After stripping off several layers of thick brown paper we came upon an enormous chunk of Ruža's home-cured pig and some hard spicy sausages of gargantuan proportions, of the type that would bring tears of joy to her daughter's eyes. There were also several packets of Croatian coffee and *Vegetat* (a substance for making soup which Katica was quite unable to find in England), and two bottles, one of *šljivovic* and the other of home-made lemonade; and finally, some hand-knitted garments for her grandchildren, and four pairs of beautiful woollen sock-slippers for Dick and me.

"Well, there you are!" I said – or something equally profound.

We both felt very humble and ashamed of our suspicions. I struggled to wrap up the parcel again, to make it look as neat as before we had begun to tamper with it.

"Come to think of it," Dick murmured thoughtfully; "I wouldn't mind being on the receiving end of those sausages myself!"

Chapter 20 - Farewell to Croatia

The telephone rang before breakfast. Dick picked up the receiver and an agitated voice announced that Zvonko wished to speak to him urgently on a matter of great importance. Dick could not understand what he was trying to tell him, and neither could I till I persuaded him to speak very slowly – *polako, polako* – and repeat each word so that I could translate it to my husband.

Zvonko wanted us to come over to Lovran for a private interview immediately, he told me, and it took some quick thinking and a few big lies to circumvent him. "We've made arrangements to meet Janja and Filip," I blustered; "so we shall not be here for much of the day. But Dick is coming over to fetch you at six o'clock, and there will be plenty of time to talk this evening."

"What I wish to say is PRIVATE," he emphasized; "and not for the ears of all the others."

"Well, I expect we could manage a private talk in a corner of the lounge – I'm sure the others wouldn't mind," I suggested hopefully. Then, in case he should think up some new scheme, I continued hastily; "Thank you very much for our lovely presents. I love my two cushion covers – they are SO pretty – also the little Chinese scent-spray and brush-holder. And Dick is delighted with his bottle of wine. So sorry, but I have to go now or we shall be late. *Do vidjenja!*"

"Phew!" I sank down into a soft chair beside Dick on the balcony, and we discussed how best to cope with Zvonko that evening so that his private worries did not overshadow the whole party.

Friday, April 12th, was meant to be our leisure day – a day for buying presents to take home, for exploring Opatija and for doing our packing – and, as a grand finale, for giving our dinner-party in the evening. It was a blue and gold morning and the handsome nineteenth century Austrian villas drowsed in the foreground, surrounded by dark green cypresses, umbrella pines, fig trees – everything bursting into life. The sapphire and gold sea sang a gentle lullaby below us, and far away across the Gulf, the blue mountains sang a different song to a gleaming blue sky dotted with sunbeams.

We strolled down into the town and watched the women along the sea-walls doing their *ručni rad*, with their beautiful work spread out all round them. We discovered a small promontory covered in fir trees, with the bronze figure of a girl in a wind-clinging dress holding a seagull on her outstretched hand. She stood on an outlying rock at the far end, and a pair of Chinese students were busy photographing each other, posing carefully so as to include the girl in the background.

"Plees, you take me and my fliend together?" invited one of the youths, handing me his camera.

Further on we came to some shops where we bought Croatian souvenirs, local coffee and balls of thread for crochet-work for our friends in England; also a gigantic Teddy Bear for Baby Marija. The three of us lunched at an open-air café near the market-place, then we strolled back to the Hotel Admiral, did our packing and had a short nap.

Dick was due to set off about half past five to pick up Anica and her three children and Zvonko from Lovran. Her sister could not leave the hospital, but Ante and his wife and baby were coming on foot. We were still dozing fitfully on our bed when the telephone rang.

"Yes?" I grabbed the receiver. "Who's there?"

"Zvonko is here!" a deep male voice shattered my calm; "And I wish to speak to you."

"Well, I'm here," I snapped peevishly.

"Not on the telephone, but in person," the voice demanded. "I am here in Opatija."

"Whereabouts?" I asked in a state of panic.

"In your hotel, close to the reception desk."

"But Dick was coming over to fetch you ... never mind, we'll be down very soon."

"He certainly knows how to get his own way," Dick remarked, as we dressed hastily and combed our hair, then took the lift to the ground floor. "I'll stay with you as long as possible before going to fetch Anica, and we'll try to find out what's on his mind."

Zvonko stood up to greet us, looking very smart in a dark suit with a white shirt and beige waistcoat. But the moment he started to share with us his *problema*, I knew that I was hopelessly lost. A torrent of words poured over my head while he fixed me with a stern look – eyeball to eyeball again, and no escape.

Dick had a sudden inspiration: "Let's ask our friend in Reception to translate for us," he suggested, pulling the reluctant Zvonko towards the desk.

Once the initial shyness had worn off and Zvonko saw that the man wished to help him, we settled down to a three-sided conversation that soon exposed the big *problema* – something that had never occurred to us in our wildest dreams.

"Because my daughter, Ivana, has drawn this picture of a Croatian village being shelled by the enemy, and it is on exhibition in a famous museum in London for all the world to see, I fear that some Serbs will also see it and track down my child to kill her?"

We had brought him a copy of the drawing, thinking that he would be so proud of Ivana, and it took a great deal of reasoning on our part, helped by the head of Reception, to persuade poor Zvonko that there was unlikely to be any danger because life in England was quite different, and those sort of crimes just did not happen there.

Ante Marić, his wife, Anica, and Baby Marija arrived at that moment, so we sat them down with Zvonko in a corner of the lounge and ordered drinks at the bar; then Dick rushed out to fetch the others from Lovran. Zvonko, I was relieved to see, had calmed down and appeared to have accepted our soothing words. And the business of introducing Marija to the bear, whose head was twice as big as her own, occupied most of our time until the rest of the party joined us.

Anica was wearing the blue and black costume with brass buttons that I had brought her from London. Mira had lent her sister her best white lace blouse, and she looked very elegant surrounded by Antonija, Marjan and Josip, who gazed at their mother with deep admiration. Dick was wearing his last clean shirt and a bow-tie with racing-cars flashing across it, and an air of excitement gripped the whole party as we left the lounge and walked down two flights of stairs. It was just then that I began to pray for peace and calmness in the dining-room, no more dramas with Zvonko and no nastiness from the head-waiter nor the waitresses!

Well, the nine adults, one baby and one large Teddy Bear advanced into that vast crowded room, and then the most extraordinary things began to happen. First of all the senior waitress, a stout matron with auburn hair and the eyes of an eagle, came running towards us with her arms outstretched. She seized the baby from her mother and twirled her round in mid air, held firmly aloft, while she cooed and clucked and called Marija a precious angel, and the baby gurgled and laughed and pulled her hair. By that time there were at least six waitresses queuing up to pet the baby and kiss our guests and, finally, the head-waiter himself appeared on the scene and uttered words like "*Zdravo!*" and "*Dobro došli*! (Welcome!)" and "What a fine baby you have!"

The joyful noises all round our table were quite deafening, and it was not until an elderly German tourist, using his knife as a gavel, gave three thunderous bangs on his table and roared for service, that the hubbub began to subside. Ante told us that some of the waitresses were old friends of theirs, as they used to work in the Hotel Zagreb and had known his wife when she was pregnant, but this was the first time they had seen Marija – hence all the excitement.

We were treated like royalty that evening, and I began to feel quite sorry for the hung-over Danes and the angry Germans. The menu was clearly a source of pure joy to all our guests, and Zvonko the squire was back in business, passing the bread basket and helping to pour out the wine.

Dick and I sat in central positions on either side of the long table with our friends all around us. I do not remember what we ate or drank, only that it was a serenely happy evening, a time for nostalgic memories and brave plans for the future. We drank to absent friends, and peace in a normal world, forgetting for a while the nightmares so close at hand. An extra chair had been drawn up so that the bear could sit next to Marija; and when she grew sleepy, Ante held her in his arms and rocked her gently to and fro.

A number of unexpected treats came our way towards the end of dinner: extra large liqueurs and brandies, delicious sweets and chocolates, various creamy cakes and slices of cheese with grapes that we had no recollection of having ordered. Even one of the chefs came out of his kitchen to assist at our departure. What with the head-waiter, wine-waiter and most of the waitresses, and all the kissing and clucking and gurgling, and the *"Do vidjenjas"* and *"Sretan puts"*, it was quite a send-off. And in the middle of it all I had a jewel of an idea!

"Why don't we go upstairs to our room now, and ring up Marica at Thoresby?" I suggested.

"I haven't spoken to my sister for over a year," Ante was the first to react. "It would be the perfect way to end such a perfect evening!"

Some of us squeezed into the lift while the children ran up the stairs, and a few minutes later all ten of us plus the bear were crowded into our untidy bedroom. The grown-ups and baby sat on the bed and the children stood on the balcony gazing at the lights of Rijeka across the bay. I dialled the vital numbers and, simultaneously, I began to suffer from serious qualms. Supposing she's out or we can't get through, I thought to myself in desperation; then all this will be nothing but a sad disappointment.

Marijana's voice came on the line two minutes later – rather faint and nervous in far-away England. Who on earth would call them at that time of night?

It was such a wonderful moment when she realized who was there.

Everyone spoke to Marica, Marijana, Ivana and sleepy little Damir at Thoresby, and for a few magic moments it seemed as if there were fourteen of us all together in that room, instead of ten. Zvonko held back till everyone else had spoken, then we left him alone on the bed with the telephone clasped in his hands, while we crowded on to the balcony under the glittering starry sky.

"This has been an evening I shall not forget," declared Josip, his teeth gleaming in the darkness. And next to him Baby Marija gurgled happily in her mother's arms.

* * * * * *

We left Opatija at nine o'clock next morning, and we needed the help of two porters to trundle all our luggage across the road to the place where the car was parked.

The bill for our dinner-party came to less than for any previous party we had given during the past few years and the Hotel Admiral, in those three short days, had come to feel like a home from home. Saying goodbye to the girls upstairs, the dining-room staff and the head of Reception was quite a wrench, and I found myself envying the plump Germans tourists who had many more days of placid holiday life stretching ahead of them!

We drove steeply upwards through the rugged mountains of Istria, then across the frontier into Slovenia. The Citroen was waved through the barrier by a couple of bored soldiers – no passport control, nor custom's officers ferreting in our luggage. All the bottles of *raki* and *Prošek* and lavender oil from Hvar, and others from Brač and Istria clanked together optimistically inside a big cardboard box in which we had installed them on the back seat.

"Let's hope every frontier is like this one," I murmured to Dick, "because we still have four more to cross."

The main road running across the centre of Slovenia seemed rather ugly and dull. We moved very slowly in a long line of trucks and lorries, and the hills were half-covered in melting snow with depressed-looking towns sprawling over the plateau beneath them. We joined the *autobahn* at Postojna, and after that we were travelling so fast that the scenery became little more than a grey blur or a long tunnel through the heart of the Alps.

The frontier between Slovenia and Austria passed without incident. We stopped for lunch in a well-stocked *autobahn* cafeteria, then drove north-west until we ran into a snowstorm south of Salzburg.

"We'll carry on till six o'clock," Dick announced, peering through the silent snowflakes with red-rimmed eyes. "By that time I reckon I'll have driven far enough and you'd better look at the map and pick somewhere to spend the night."

We were not far from Munich at half past five, so I suggested trying a village on the shores of one of the Bavarian lakes.

"That sounds fine," Dick agreed; "as long as it's not one of the big tourist resorts."

"There's a lake called the Starnberger See about ten minutes' drive from here, and I've never heard of it before," I told him. "Let's try this little village called Ammerland? It might have an inn, and it's the same name as one of our favourite Dutch islands."

"As good a reason as any!" he laughed, beginning to enjoy the beautiful countryside away from the stressful *autobahn*.

The Hotel Am See on the east shore of the Starnberger See at Ammerland turned out to be just perfect. The landlord gave us a charming room furnished in the old Bavarian style, and dinner that night was served by an elderly waiter who painted for us a brilliant picture of life on the shores of the lake as he remembered it in the days of his youth.

A long pier stretched out into the lake, where a steamer called from time to time. We stood at the far end after breakfast next morning, gazing at the snowy mountains away to the south while the grey windswept water lapped noisily under our feet.

We drove north-westwards all that day, passing close to Karlsruhe, crossing the Rhine at Aachen, then on past Metz and Verdun till we came to the neighbourhood of Reims. A lady in the tourist Advice Bureau at one of the service stations recommended us to try the Hotel du Cheval Blanc at Sept-Saulx in the heart of the Champagne region.

It was a picturesque old building set in a pretty garden with a trout stream running through it. Our room was very elegant and the dinner was certainly French *haute cuisine* at its most spectacular. But the other guests were all English – with a capital E. Squires and retired military men who spoke with parade-ground voices, enunciating each word with remarkable clarity, their wives clad in shapeless woollen garments and pearl necklaces. And ageing schoolmasters treating young gays to a champagne holiday with an educational bias.

Madame stood in the middle of her superb dining-room smiling sweetly at all her guests, while her crew of handsome young waiters used persuasive language to describe and advise on the sumptuous *á la carte* menu. I developed severe tummy-ache towards the end of dinner, and Dick said he felt sick.

"It seems a far cry from our meals in Croatia," I remarked rather sadly as we walked across the garden to our sleeping quarters that night.

The bill next morning was the largest we had paid for any one night during our journey across Europe. We drove to the old Reims motor-racing circuit after breakfast and stood in the derelict spectator's stand for a while, trying to picture some of Dick's racing heroes who had driven the course so magnificently in bygone days.

We paused again further north to visit the very moving small British cemetery at Cantaing; and to eat *croques Monsieurs* in a village *estaminet* nearby. Then we drove north to Calais and caught the afternoon ferry, THE PRIDE OF KENT, back to Dover.

I telephoned to Marica and Katica at Thoresby later that night, to tell them we were back in England and to give them messages from their families in Croatia.

"We brought home a big parcel from your mother for you, which started its journey in Krajina," I told Katica; "and we should be back at *Butterfields* by Wednesday, so we'll let you have it as soon as we get there."

"I know. She wrote and told me about the special sausages she would send me;" (I could almost see Katica smiling with pleasure at the other end of the line) "so Milan and I wish to invite you to dinner on Thursday evening, as we want to share with you all that she has sent us?"

Epilogue

Another year has passed and part of our big family is succeeding, in its various ways, to climb out of the pit of despair into a normal world in which its members can hold their heads high, hope for a better future and live like reasonable human beings once again.

The Jerbić family in Meadow Cottages was doing well. Milan and Katica each found jobs last summer – he works for the East Midland Bus Company and she has a job in a local textile factory. They earn only a few pounds more than those on the dole, but Milan would tell people; "I am very happy as I have a nice home, my family around me and my pride restored now that I need no longer receive money each week for which I have not worked. One day I hope to be promoted and to earn a better wage."

They have created a splendid vegetable garden in their spare time which is the envy of all their neighbours, and they have saved up to buy their own furniture and carpets. Natali and Ivan are happy at school and have made some good friends. She has just finished her GCSE exams, and would like to work towards a job in the legal profession when she is old enough.

Like a shell exploding out of a clear blue sky, suddenly last April Milan and Katica were summoned to East Midlands Airport for an interview with the Immigration Authorities, and told that they had not been granted asylum to stay in England. Their new-found peace has been totally shattered, they have no home to go to in any other country, and they know that Milan would probably be tortured and shot if he ever returned to Croatia.

We have found them a lawyer to take their case to Appeal, and their friends are rallying round for the dreadful moment when their next summons arrives from the Immigration Department.

Marica the home-maker still lives in the Stables' flat, and she is now greeted with pleasure by John the Bee when they meet in the courtyard; and he presented her with a pot of his own special honey last Christmas.

She, Marijana and Ivana work in the restaurant next to the Pierrepont Gallery during the busy weekends in summertime, and they help to keep our church at Perlethorpe clean and shining all through the year.

"As long as my children are happy, then so am I," she declares, although she has plenty to worry about back home: her family, who are still living in refugee hostels, Zvonko, who has joined the army now that his leg is better, and her general uncertainty about the future. Will she also receive that dreaded summons to East Midlands Airport one day soon?

Marijana celebrated her twenty-first birthday in June, and she and Robert became engaged on the same day. She also passed her English exam with top marks and has a computer certificate as well. There is no doubt that none of Marica's children wish to return to Croatia as they have all made friends at college and at school, also amongst their neighbours at Thoresby.

Janja and her family are still living in the refugee hostel at Kostrena, near Rijeka, but they telephoned us with great joy to say that they would soon be returning to their home-village in Krajina now that the Croats had won the battle for Knin.

Anica and her family have been floating on clouds since last winter, because they were able to buy their own house just before Christmas, 1994, in a small town called Podrarska Slatina not far from the Hungarian frontier. She worked extremely hard in a pizza restaurant all last summer while Anton travelled around the country whenever he could get leave from the army, searching and searching for a house they could afford.

Anica writes joyously; "At last we have a HOME again, Anton comes on leave whenever he can manage it, and we are SO happy to be all together again in our own home. I cannot describe to you what a beautiful feeling it is. We have only a few pieces of furniture and it is very cold here with much snow; but what does that matter when life is so good?"

Since that letter we have received further happy details of the flowers and fruit trees bursting into life in her garden, and the friends she and the children are making in the neighbourhood. All we can hope is that the war will not touch them in North-Eastern Croatia, and Anton will return safely to his family at the end of the war.

Baby Marija in Opatija has a brother, Marica tells us; and big John lives in Lipik most of the time now. He was caught in the middle of the fighting when the Croatian soldiers seized Pakrac from the Serbs earlier this year. He is hoping to start work on the rebuilding of another orphanage in Sarajevo, but the situation has made this impossible for the time being.

Our old friends on the Dalmatian Islands are struggling to survive. Maté died quite suddenly of heart trouble in the spring time, and Vera is quite devastated by her loss. The chances of her having a hip operation seem more remote than ever, but Jakše is still at home, thank God, although no one knows how soon he will be ordered to rejoin the army.

More than a thousand people came to Maté's funeral, and this, I imagine, has left the family without a penny to buy food or pay their bills. Little Verica had her First Communion soon after her grandfather died.

I read an interesting article in the Daily Telegraph not so long ago, about that obscure little airfield we had spotted on the central plateau of Brač last spring. Apparently, "Operation Lofty View" is being run by a twenty-strong team of American military personnel who live in Bol. Unmanned aircraft, which can fly for up to forty-eight hours, are launched by them from the airfield and are thought to be homing in on infantry and artillery concentrations, and photographing front lines and troop positions. This has heightened speculation that America is supplying the Bosnian army with intelligence. The team of Americans are shadowed by plain clothes Croatian guards, and military police turn away all visitors to the airfield.

*   *   *   *   *   *

The coming of our big family to Thoresby has been a stirring experience for us over the past three years. The whole affair was a much bigger responsibility and more time-consuming than we had ever imagined it would be; but the benefits have far outweighed those few selfish considerations. Our refugees have turned out to be not just any old people who lost their homes through no faults of their own, but SPECIAL PEOPLE who brought with them their old-fashioned standards of behaviour, their courage and simple faith. Their children, although they are now exposed to the ways of Western Europe, have changed very little, and there seems every chance that they will follow in their parents' footsteps.

We are SO lucky to be counted as their friends.